Samuel Johnson

1 Johnson in 1773
From the portrait by Reynolds

Samuel Johnson

and his Times

M. J. C. HODGART

ARCO PUBLISHING COMPANY, Inc.
NEW YORK

First published 1963 *in the United States by*
ARCO PUBLISHING COMPANY, Inc.
480 Lexington Avenue, New York 17, N.Y.

Library of Congress Catalog Card Number: 63-17095
ARCO Catalog Number: 1091

Printed in Great Britain

CONTENTS

ACKNOWLEDGMENT

The Author and Publishers wish to thank the following for permission to reproduce the illustrations included in this book:

His Grace the Duke of Buccleuch and Queensberry, for fig. 4
The Trustees of the British Museum, for figs. 13, 17, 18 and 20
The National Portrait Gallery, for figs. 3, 5, 6, 10, 12 and 14
The Master and Fellows of Pembroke College, Oxford, for fig. 16
The Trustees of the Tate Gallery, London, for fig. 1
University Library, Cambridge, for fig. 8
The Trustees of the Victoria and Albert Museum, for fig. 11
The Warburg Institute, for fig. 21

The quotation from Boswell's *London Journal* on page 65 is made by permission of the Yale Editions of the Private Papers of James Boswell, and William Heinemann Ltd.

LIST OF ILLUSTRATIONS

BIBLIOGRAPHY

ANYONE who writes a short book on Samuel Johnson must be greatly in debt to the many scholars and critics who have added to our knowledge of him. I wish to acknowledge my debt to those who appear in the following list, which is only a short selection of recent works concerning Johnson and his period; and to many others who do not appear in it for reasons of space. In particular I am grateful to the Editors of the Yale Edition of the *Boswell Papers* and to Messrs. Heinemann for permission to quote from the *London Journal*.

Samuel Johnson, *Works*, 9 vols. Oxford 1825.

The Letters of Samuel Johnson. Ed. R. W. Chapman. 3 vols. 1952.

Johnson, Prose and Poetry. Selected by Mona Wilson (text edited by John Crow) 1950.

Selections from Samuel Johnson. Edited and introduced by R. W. Chapman, 1955.

The Wisdom of Johnson: Comments on Life and Moral Precepts Chosen from his writings. Edited by Constantia Maxwell, 1948.

Samuel Johnson. *Diaries, Prayers and Annals*. Edited by E. L. McAdam, jr. with Donald and Mary Hyde. 1958. (Yale Edition of the Works of Samuel Johnson, vol. i.)

Boswell's *Life of Johnson*, edited by George Birkbeck Hill, revised by L. F. Powell, 6 vols. 1934–50.

Boswell's *London Journal, 1762–63*, edited by Frederick A. Pottle. Heinemann, 1950 (Yale Edition of Boswell Papers).

Boswell in Holland 1763–64. Ed. Pottle. 1952.

Boswell on the Grand Tour: Germany and Switzerland. Ed. Pottle. 1953.

Boswell on the Grand Tour: Italy, Corsica and France. Ed. Frank Brady and Pottle. 1955.

Boswell in Search of a Wife, 1766–69. Ed. Brady and Pottle. 1957.

Boswell for the Defence, 1769–74. Ed. W. K. Wimsatt and Pottle. 1960.

Boswell's *Journal of a Tour to the Hebrides with Samuel Johnson* LLD. Now first published from the original manuscript. Ed. Pottle and Charles H. Bennett. 1936.

Thraliana. The Diary of Mrs Hester Lynch Thrale (later Mrs Piozzi). Ed. Katharine C. Balderston. 2 vols. 1951.

Hester Lynch Piozzi, *Anecdotes of the late Samuel Johnson* LLD. 1786 (reprinted in Johnsonian Miscellanies, ed. G. B. Hill, 2 vols. 1897).

E. L. McAdam, jr., *Dr Johnson and the English Law*. 1951.

Bertrand H. Bronson, *Johnson Agonistes and other essays*. 1946.

James L. Clifford, *Hester Lynch Piozzi* (Mrs Thrale). 1941.

James L. Clifford, *Young Samuel Johnson*. 1955.

S. C. Roberts, *The Story of Dr Johnson*. 1919.

S. C. Roberts, 'Johnson'. (*Proceedings of the British Academy xxx.*) 1944.

W. K. Wimsatt, *The Prose Style of Johnson*. 1941.

W. K. Wimsatt, *Philosophic Words:* A Study of Style and Meaning in the 'Rambler' and Dictionary of Johnson. 1948.

Ian Watt, 'Samuel Johnson: the Literature of Experience', *The Listener*, Sept. 1959.

The Age of Johnson. Essays presented to Chauncey Brewster Tinker. 1949.

New Light on Dr Johnson. Essays on the occasion of his 250th Birthday. Edited by Frederick W. Hilles. 1959.

Johnson's England. Ed. A. S. Turberville. 1933.

T. F. Ashton, *An Economic History of England in the Eighteenth Century*. 1955.

W. G. Hoskins, *The Making of the English Landscape*. 1955.

Leon Radzinowicz, *A History of English Criminal Law and its Administration from 1750*. Vol. I: *The Movement for Reform*. 1948.

Chapter I

LICHFIELD

I LICHFIELD

1709–1737

'A MIND of large general powers, accidentally directed to some particular direction': such is Samuel Johnson's description of 'genius'. Johnson's own mind, however, possessing the largest general powers of all but a few in British history, was exercised in many directions. He was first and foremost a poet, and his poetic imagination illuminates his prose and dazzles in his conversation, which is the most splendid ever recorded. He was the first great lexicographer of his language, and the *Dictionary* remained supreme for over a century. He was one of the best literary critics of all time, and there is no better short biography than his life of Savage. He was a fine scholar, both in the Classics and in the history of English literature. Debarred by his lack of a university degree from entering any of the learned professions, of which he would have preferred Law, he acquired a vast amount of professional learning. He was the most distinguished layman-lawyer of his day, giving practical help to his legal friends and affecting the later reform of the English criminal law. His interest in and knowledge of politics were also considerable. Deeply religious, he was also a notable layman-divine, not indeed a speculative theologian, but a great churchman and a generous writer of other men's sermons. Of the third profession, Medicine, he again probably knew as much as any layman of his day. His interest in medicine was linked with his study of natural science, or 'philosophy', as he called it: he read widely in the great scientists of the previous century and was a keen experimenter in chemistry. From science he went on to technology, and was praised by the inventor Arkwright as having a unique grasp of the principles of machinery. He had a good understanding of the theory of commerce as well as of its practice: he helped to run Thrale's brewery with the practical efficiency he had shown in Thrale's election campaigns. The only subject he can be said to have neglected was metaphysics. His refutation of Bishop Berkeley's idealism by kicking the stone was hardly a logical refutation, but it was a magnificent gesture. Above all, he knew men. He understood his own mind very well, and, less egotistical than most men of genius, could grasp intuitively the complex characters of his friends, who included the first minds of the age. Applying insight and intelligence to the problems of the moral life, and conveying his immense experience in memorable aphorisms, he became a teacher of wisdom to his own and to later generations.

Yet Johnson himself was dissatisfied with his achievements. Even at the end of a long and busy life, with a vast amount of work behind him, he thought that he had wasted much of his time: year after year, in his *Prayers and Meditations*, he confesses to idleness and promises to do better. This was not morbid self-laceration. He knew that, since he had been able to do so much, he could have done even more. What he did, however, has been the subject of hundreds of books, from Boswell's to the present day, to which I must declare my debt. I have not tried to compete with the many excellent psychological or literary studies which are easily available; instead, I have tried to relate Johnson to the age in which he lived, and to say what he means, or could mean, to ours. In his multifarious interests, Johnson was very much a man of his century; a century in which the world was transformed by British inventors, industrialists, statesmen, soldiers, essayists and poets. What we can learn from the past is always limited, since our problems are always new ones. But Johnson both created and transmitted some of the ideals of eighteenth-century civilization which are most valuable to us today: the ideals of independence, energy, and frankness, which I should like to hope have had some part in the making of this book.

Johnson, who 'had, till his very death, a contempt for the notion that the weather affects the human frame', was born in the bad year

1709, on the 18th of September (the 7th by the old-style calendar). The winter of 1708–9 had been severe, the summer wet and cold, the harvest very poor; since it had been little better in the previous summer, prices rose, there were food riots in some places, and a general spread of disease, which is reflected in the rising number of burials. Johnson's family were not poor enough to suffer from privation, but it is possible that Sam's health suffered from the spread of disease caused by the malnutrition of his poorer neighbours. Taken to a wet nurse, he returned in a few weeks 'a poor, diseased infant, almost blind'. He had developed tubercular glands, or scrofula, the scars of which he carried on his neck to the end of his life. That this may be of significance is shown by a remark of Samuel Taylor Coleridge, who resembled Johnson in so many ways; although Coleridge is thinking only of himself, and although his medical lore may not amount to much, this is a remarkable description of Johnson's type: 'Where you find a man indolent in body & indisposed to definite action, but with lively Feelings, vivid ideal Images, & a power & habit of continuous Thinking, you may always, I believe, suspect a somewhat of Scrofula.'

This was to be the last bad harvest for some years, and for most of Johnson's life the weather smiled on the farmers of England and consequently on the many poor who lived so near the subsistence level that they suffered when the price of corn rose. There were poor harvests only in 1727–29, '39–40, '51–53, '56, '64, '66–68, '72–74, and '82–84, but during the other years the weather was apparently above average. This was important, since the England into which Johnson was born lived by agriculture. Trade was large and increasing, but the Industrial Revolution had emphatically not begun. Most of the country's wealth was in land, and the landed classes were in the ascendancy, socially and politically. Although rents were rising, agriculture was relatively inefficient, except in a few areas like Norfolk. About two million acres of modern farming land had not yet been reclaimed; while of the land under cultivation, half was enclosed and half was still on the open-field system. The amount of enclosure varied greatly from one part of the country to the next: much of the south-east and the west had been enclosed for two centuries, but the Midlands were still largely open-field. The country of south Staffordshire, around Lichfield, was half enclosed, while around the town itself were open fields, cultivated in long strips, on which the burgesses had the right to pasture their cattle—consequently enclosure was often resisted by the members of small town corporations. Here Johnson would not have noticed great changes during his lifetime, but farther south, on his journeys to and from Birmingham and London, he must have seen the modern landscape develop, especially after the middle of the century: with new hedges, straight roads, farm-houses out in the fields instead of huddled in villages, better breeds of stock in the rolling acres of Warwickshire, new crops like turnips to feed the stock in winter, new palaces for the rich, set in immense parks.

But Johnson cared for little of this. He was a townsman, sometimes bored with his farming friend Taylor, whose 'talk is of bullocks'; he believed that 'no wise man will go to live in the country unless he has something to do which can be better done in the country'. The town he knew first was a small cathedral city, with a population of about two thousand, which would hardly be reckoned as more than a village today. It was run by two bodies, the Cathedral chapter and the corporation, both self-electing bodies with more privileges than practical functions and, like most similar bodies in the eighteenth century, in a moribund state. The Johnsons had little to do with the Cathedral officers; the Bishops were usually absent, and Gilbert Walmsley, a rich friend, had leased the Bishop's Palace. But Johnson's father was a member of the corporation, and held at one time or another most of the important posts: sheriff in 1709 and one of the Brethren and magistrates in 1712. It was an old-fashioned community, traditionally High Church, Tory and Jacobite, although there were no signs of disloyalty during the Rebellion of 1715. Johnson remained proud of his citizenship.

Johnson's was the classic background to a successful literary career: a poorish but educated home in the provinces. His father was a bookseller, who came up a good deal in the world and then sank again, because of financial difficulties. From him Sam inherited his vast body and his congenital melancholy; and in the shop he educated himself, tearing the heart out of hundreds of books. Sam's mother was of gentler birth; the Fords had landed connexions, among them 'Parson' Cornelius Ford, rake and wit, who had a great influence on Sam. There is, however, nothing to explain the birth of such a prodigy, on genetic grounds. The parents were elderly when Sam was born, but produced another son three years later, Nathaniel, who died in obscurity at twenty-four. Sam had the kind of devotion to his mother that sickly children usually develop; but there is not enough evidence to justify an Oedipean explanation of his neurosis.

Johnson was not one of those writers who draw on their childhood experience.[1] What little he cared to remember of his childhood he put down in a few pages of his *Annals*: the most notable event was his being 'taken to London to be touched for the evil by Queen Anne', in one of the last Royal attempts to be made at the faith-healing of scrofula. He wrote down no account of the Queen but told Mrs Thrale 'he thought he had some confused Remembrance of a Lady in a black Hood'.[2] The house in which he was born and continued to live was large and solid, built before the family affairs started to go downhill. Despite his very poor eyesight and bad health, Sam's education began early and proceeded. From Dame Oliver's school he went at eight to Lichfield Grammar School —an excellent school which sent many boys to Oxford and thence into the professions, especially law. Two years later he entered the upper school, where he learned Latin under the ferocious Hunter: 'My master whipped me very well. Without that, Sir, I should have done nothing.' He could have learned little but Latin at school, unless he had been sent to one of the Dissenting academies; but his reading must have gone on at home on a large scale. At sixteen he had taken all that the Grammar School had to offer, and left to spend some months with Parson Ford at Pedmore near Stourbridge. If he had been of a rich family he would probably have gone up to Oxford at this age; but he learned from Ford, who had been in the London literary world, something that neither school nor university could provide: a taste for wit and general knowledge.

> Nealy Ford [he told Mrs Thrale] advised him to study the Principles of every thing, that a general Acquaintance with Life might be the Consequence of his Enquiries—Learn said he the leading Precognita of all things—no need perhaps to turn over leaf by leaf; but grasp the Trunk hard only, and you will shake all the Branches.

[1] His early life has been so well described by J. L. Clifford in *Young Samuel Johnson*, Heinemann, 1955, that little need be said here.

[2] *Thraliana*, p. 160; Mrs Thrale later added 'and Diamonds', *Anecdotes*, p. 152.

From this time Sam began to develop his immense grasp of all kinds of subjects and his powers as a conversationalist.

In 1726 he spent a few months at Stourbridge school, apparently as an assistant master (entering a profession in which he was to prove a notable failure), and then for two years he helped his father with the bookshop, and with the book-stalls and auctions he went all over the Midlands. During this time he received further encouragement to pursue the study of polite letters and to practise the art of conversation from Gilbert Walmsley, to whose piety and learning he paid tribute in the *Lives of the Poets*. Walmsley was a violent Whig, and Sam already a violent Tory, but since the older man admired forthrightness they remained friends. At last, apparently by the happy chance of legacy to Mrs Johnson, came Sam's opportunity to go to Oxford. His reason for wanting to go there was not only to learn more classics—at nineteen he had about as much Latin as he would ever have and that was a great deal—but his knowledge of Greek needed improvement. It was also that a university degree was a necessary qualification for entering any of the professions, not only law, which was his first choice, but even schoolmastering, as Sam found to his cost. Oxford, sunk in prejudice and port, was entirely agreeable to Johnson: indeed he gloried in the prejudice, High Church or Jacobite, and had no objection to the port. He always defended his university against the well-justified charges of sloth, and did not care if his tutors had nothing to teach him. The reasons for the almost complete collapse of the English universities in the early eighteenth century are by no means clear. It was not a matter of politics: Cambridge, which enjoyed more of the favour of the Whig ruling class, also suffered a similar decline: the number of undergraduates fell off sharply from the late seventeenth century. That had also been a brilliant period of scholarship, especially in historical studies; but for some reason research became unfashionable, and there were few scholars of repute left in the universities, apart from Cambridge's Bentley. In the dilettante atmosphere of Georgian times, 'culture' tended to be prized above solid learning. Nor was teaching any better than research. Few of the professors bothered to give lectures, leaving them to their juniors, but then, as Johnson said, with some truth, 'Lectures were once useful; but now, when all can read, and books are so numerous, lectures are

2 Lichfield in 1785. On the right is the house where Johnson was born
Engraved from a drawing by E. Stringer

3 David Garrick
From a pencil drawing attributed to George Dance

unnecessary.' Instruction was based, as now, largely on the tutorial system, but the tutors tended to be of low calibre. They were mostly very young clergymen, waiting eagerly for rich livings which would allow them to get married. Oxford and Cambridge had become finishing schools for the sons of the rich, noblemen or gentlemen-commoners who would dine with the Fellows on High Table at the age of fifteen or sixteen.

Still, this was the gateway into life, and for every young man the October day when he comes up is the day of rebirth, when, as has been said, death seems farthest away. Within a few weeks Johnson had committed what to dons is the most unforgivable sin: he had cut his tutorial, to go sliding in Christ Church meadow. When reprimanded he showed nonchalance. BOSWELL: 'That, Sir, was great fortitude of mind.' JOHNSON: 'No, Sir; stark insensibility.' Sam was indeed an irreverent rebel, famous for his wit and academic brilliance. 'Ah, Sir, I was rude and violent. It was bitterness which they mistook for frolic.' He was not badly off at first: he possessed a personal library of a hundred books, and did not have to work his way through college as a batteler or servitor, waiting on his fellow-undergraduates. But after little more than a year of continuous residence his money began to run out, a promise of help from a schoolfellow having come to nothing. In December 1729 he left for Lichfield to see if anything could be done about his future: but the family finances were now in a hopeless state. Although he kept his name on the books of Pembroke College for some months, he did not return to Oxford until the years of fame.

His prospects apparently blasted, Johnson suffered the first serious attack of the mental illness that plagued his life. He called it 'a vile melancholy', which 'made him mad all his life, at least not sober'. It would seem to have been an acute anxiety neurosis, accompanied by an intolerable sense of guilt and the fear of permanent madness. From this time probably began the twitchings and compulsive movements which alarmed everyone who met him for the first time: Johnson, for example, could never cross a threshold without a long pause followed by a violent jump. Johnson's life was to be a heroic struggle against his physical and mental disabilities, but in 1730 he was out of action, overwhelmed as Boswell describes it, 'with an horrible hypochondria, with perpetual irritation, fretfulness and impatience, and with a dejection, gloom, and despair, which made existence misery'. In the intervals of illness, he helped with the shop, went on reading and talking in the Walmsley circle. There he found a new friend in Cornet Harry Hervey, a young rake: 'a vicious man, but very kind to me. If you call a dog HERVEY, I shall love him'. When some years later Hervey, like Alec D'Urberville, took to religion, Johnson wrote his inaugural sermon for him. At the end of 1731 Michael Johnson died, leaving his son only £20 and his wife little but his failing business. Sam again tried schoolmastering for a few months, and then in 1733 went to stay with his old friend Edmund Hector in Birmingham. He entered a cosy lower-middle-class circle which included his future wife, a woman in her forties then married to a Mr Porter, a mercer. Everyone that knew Johnson was convinced that he was a genius, lost in sloth. Johnson had a good deal in common with S. T. Coleridge, and Hector with Coleridge's kind host, Gillman, who kept trying to get him to write his Shakespeare lectures. Johnson was so lazy that he would only write lying in bed, while Hector took down from dictation a translation of Father Lobo's book on Abyssinia; and thanks to Hector this book was published in 1735. It had no success, and is only remarkable for showing that Johnson's mature style and outlook were fully formed in his twenties. He holds forth, for example, on primitivism and the myth of the Noble Savage, about which he was still arguing with Boswell forty years later:

> The reader will here find no regions cursed with irremediable barrenness, or blessed with spontaneous fecundity; no perpetual gloom, or unceasing sunshine; nor are the nations here described either devoid of all sense of humanity, or consummate in all private and social virtues.

There is something both ludicrous and tragic about Johnson in this Birmingham setting and indeed throughout his twenties: he can be pictured as a kind of Mr Polly or Kipps, but just as easily as a Jude the Obscure, his 'worth by poverty depressed'. Everything about his marriage is wholly grotesque except one thing: Johnson admired Mrs Porter ('Tetty') for her intelligence and always valued her literary judgment. He married her in 1735, within a year of her husband's death; she was over twenty years older than he was. They had seventeen years of married life, most of which were years of unhappiness for them both. The impression Boswell gives is almost certainly wrong: Johnson sentimentalized her memory, commemorating the anniversaries of her death in his diaries in pathetic tones, and Boswell piously repeated the myth. All the other testimony points to the opposite. Garrick, who knew her well, described her as 'very fat, with a bosom of more than ordinary protuberance, with swelled cheeks, of a florid red, produced by thick painting, and increased by the liberal use of cordials'. Her drinking grew worse in later years, when she also took to opium; though she was jealous of other women, she banished her husband from her bed for many years. She had a little money, which they spent on opening a boarding school at Edial near Lichfield: this had only three pupils and closed within a year, when the money was gone. One of the pupils was David Garrick, who used to give a famous imitation of the pair: Johnson sitting by the bed writing his tragedy *Irene*, heedless of his wife's entreaties and absent-mindedly stuffing the bedclothes into his breeches.

When there was nothing else for it, Johnson set out for London, in March 1737, with little in his pocket except his half-finished tragedy. Garrick went with him, to go to a new school, and they shared one horse between them. Johnson was forced, at the age of twenty-seven, to enter the occupation of journalism, of which he became one of the greatest glories.

Chapter 2

LONDON

2 LONDON

1737–1746

Typically, on arriving in London, Johnson did nothing. For five or six months he hung around, admiring the sights and being entertained by Harry Hervey. He must have had some promise of work, and he must have known that London was to be his home, for in the late autumn he went back to fetch Tetty up to Town. Then, as they moved from one dingy set of lodging to another, began the first creative period of Johnson's life; and he began it by writing a satire on the place he loved best in the world.

London, then as now, was too big. With a population of half a million, it held a tenth of the inhabitants of England. Most of its people still lived in the City, while Westminster, the seat of the Court and the Government, was still distinct; but there was a steady creeping of houses towards the west and north. London was probably the greatest port in the world, and the Thames with thousands of small boats was an internal as well as an external waterway. It was a city of merchants, many of whom still lived above their shops; of small-scale manufacture, largely of luxury goods; of finance and banking. There were vast numbers of domestic servants, possibly one in five of the population; and many of the employees in trade and industry stood in the relation of servants to their employers. Both servants and apprentices were in a real sense part of the family: London, like the rest of England, was still a community of families, until the Industrial Revolution, at the end of Johnson's life, finally disintegrated the ancient patriarchal system. The system was, however, beginning to break down in Johnson's youth; and despite his hierarchical views he gloried in the freedom that the 'dissolution of dependence' in a city could give, even if this meant that the 'mob' were famous for their insolence. There was no proletariat in the modern sense: the mob consisted of the more turbulent part of the community, unemployed servants, apprentices, independent journeymen, whose normal way of calling attention to their grievances was to riot, and they would riot as often on the Tory side as on the Whig.

It is now fashionable for historians to stress the dirt, disease, crime, and other social evils of eighteenth-century London; and by now the image of elegant Georgian living, of periwigs and minuets, will have been replaced in many readers' minds by one of Hogarth's Gin Lane. Of course, London was a dirty place, its streets full of garbage and its air fouled by Newcastle coal burning in a hundred thousand open fires. There was just enough municipal hygiene to prevent a recurrence of the bubonic plague, but not enough to keep down epidemics of typhus and typhoid (London was spared the horrors of cholera until the introduction of the water-closet). Tuberculosis and the diseases of childhood were endemic. There was said to be no third generation of true Londoners, the population being kept up only by an influx of country people and Irish: those who grew up were tough.

> BOSWELL: 'I believe, Sir, a great many of the children born in London die early.' JOHNSON: 'Why, yes, Sir.' BOSWELL: 'But those who do live, are as stout and strong people as any: Dr Price says, they must be naturally strong to get through.' JOHNSON: 'That is system, sir. . . .'

Johnson may have been complacent about infant mortality, but he wrote in 1741:

> The most disgusting part of the character given by travellers, of the most savage nations, is their neglect of cleanliness, of which, perhaps, no part of the world affords more proofs than the streets of the British capital; a city famous for wealth, and commerce, and plenty, and for every other kind of civility and politeness, but which abounds with such heaps of filth as a savage would look on with amazement. . . .

Crime was increasing, as we shall see from Johnson's thoughtful treatment of this subject; and gin-drinking, with its appalling train of evils, was on the increase until 1751. Nevertheless it was possible for the average man to live a much better life in London than in the provinces. Most Londoners managed to live in peace and in a gradually increasing prosperity. It was not a world of rapid change: everything was more or less static, the death-rate, exports and imports, technology; but slowly, among a few thousand ingenious inventors and entrepreneurs, the conditions were being prepared for the astonishing explosion of capitalism which began in the last two years of Johnson's life.

To the observer of the human scene, London was the most interesting place in the world, such was the 'magnitude and variety' of life it offered. Johnson must have felt in his youth what he said thirty years later: 'The happiness of London is not to be conceived but by those who have been in it. I will venture to say, there is more learning and science within the circumference of ten miles from where we now sit, than in all the rest of the kingdom.' What Johnson enjoyed most of all was precisely that Grub Street, the world of hacks and Bohemians, which all literary men who had escaped from it despised. Nowhere else could he meet such brilliant talkers as the poet Savage, George Psalmanazar the 'Formosan' impostor, or Samuel Boyse, the most singular journalist of all, who 'laid out the last half-guinea he possessed in truffles and mushrooms, eating them in bed too, for want of clothes, or even a shirt to sit up in'. Around Grub Street was the great network of taverns and coffee houses, where at very little expense a young poet could join in conversations on a hundred subjects and enjoy the freemasonry of the well-informed. 'It is wonderful, Sir, what is to be found in London. The most literary conversation that I ever enjoyed, was at the table of Jack Ellis, a money-scrivener behind the Royal Exchange, with whom I at one period used to dine generally once a week.'

Within a few months of his arrival in this demi-Paradise Johnson wrote an attack on it, in his satire *London*. If he had died at thirty, this alone would have been remembered. It is an adaptation in modern terms of a famous satire by Juvenal, and it is no more sincere in its farewell to city life than Juvenal is. Juvenal is deeply attached to the city in which he says it is impossible to live, although he feels deeply about social evils, and protests against the fact that there is one law for the rich and another for the poor; he also gives a sharply visual picture of life in Rome, from the pigeons nesting among the roof-tiles to the brutal soldiery in the streets. He had been much imitated by English poets (Oldham, Dryden, Gay, even Swift and Pope owed much to him), who took London as their theme, and so Johnson was not being very original in producing yet another modernization of Juvenal's Third Satire. Johnson, because of his eyesight, is not strong on visual detail, but, heightening Juvenal's moral indignation, adds something which is absent from Juvenal or his imitators, a strongly political content. *London* is intimately connected with the politics of the 'thirties, that is with the long rule of Sir Robert Walpole, whom Johnson and others accused of 'corruption at home and appeasement abroad', in Sir Sydney Roberts's phrase. The politics of the poem are opposition-Whig, rather than Tory, as Clifford has pointed out: old-fashioned Toryism counted for little now, and Johnson allied himself with the Bolingbroke-Pulteney 'Craftsman' group, to which Pope was also supplying philosophical ammunition. Johnson's politics are to be taken seriously and the poem should be read as a polemical tract, with the kind of distortion that everyone thinks is justified in political warfare. Johnson was writing 'for victory' and cannot resist comic exaggeration:

> *Scarce can our Fields, such Crowds at* Tyburn *die,*
> *With Hemp the Gallows and the Fleet supply*

or ludicrous couplings:

> *Here falling Houses thunder on your Head,*
> *And here a female Atheist talks you dead.*

Although the poem lacks the grandeur and rich texture of the *Vanity of Human Wishes*, it rises to a sombre intensity when it concerns the subject Johnson knew best—poverty.

> *Has Heaven reserv'd, in Pity to the Poor,*
> *No pathless Waste, or undiscovered Shore?*
> *No secret Island in the boundless Main?*
> *No peaceful Desart yet unclaim'd by SPAIN?*
> *Quick let us rise, the happy Seats explore,*
> *And bear Oppression's Insolence no more.*
> *This mournful Truth is ev'ry where confest,*
> *SLOW RISES WORTH, BY POVERTY DEPREST.*

4 Whitehall in the mid-eighteenth century
A detail from a painting by Antonio Canaletto

5 *From a portrait after Reynolds*

6 *From the unfinished portrait by James Barry*

No one except perhaps Johnson's disciple Goldsmith has ever played the Popean tune on the heroic couplet with such skill; and Pope was impressed, saying of the unknown author 'he will soon be déterré'. If Johnson was not dug out of his sett and turned into a tame badger, it was because he did not choose to be: from idleness or Bohemianism he preferred not to pay court to a noble lord, and enter polite society as nearly all the poets before him had done. He remained in Grub Street, working for the *Gentleman's Magazine*. Edward Cave, its founder, was until 1745 the most important figure in Johnson's life: mean to the journalists he employed, he had a strange hold over them, perhaps because of the enthusiasm he showed in building up the circulation and reputation. In 1738 Johnson became one of Cave's chief assistants, taking over among other jobs the imaginative reconstruction of the proceedings of Parliament, or 'Debates in the Senate of Lilliput' on which the magazine made its name. Since Parliament refused to allow official reporters, Cave thought of introducing the speakers under easily deciphered Gulliverian names, and thus just avoiding prosecution. The debates were written up from only slight hints, and Johnson invented what he thought the speakers ought to have said. The result was often as admirable as Thucydides' or Tacitus' imaginary oratory, and the speeches were often reprinted as the genuine words of, say, Walpole or Pitt. Since the Members found themselves talking such good sense and in such noble style, on a variety of general questions which they probably never thought of, they did not make any protest, and Johnson kept the secret of his deception for some twenty years. But, when the company at Foote's were quoting with high praise a famous speech of Pitt's, Johnson came out of his silence to say, 'That speech I wrote in a garret in Exeter Street.' Although Johnson revealed the secret to his friends, the truth about the Parliamentary speeches did not soon become generally known: the speeches were often reprinted as the works of their supposed authors over the next century or longer. Thus Johnson can be said to have set to his contemporaries the standard of Parliamentary oratory and statesmanship, and to have left to posterity a flattering picture of eighteenth-century attainments in this field.

This was only one of the many tasks Johnson undertook for

Cave's modest hire. In 1738 he was working on a translation, with commentary, of Crousaz's commentary on Du Resnel's translation of Pope's *Essay on Man*—which, with the exception of a modern edition of the work (now in hand), is about as great a distance between literature and life as is possible to imagine. Johnson, however, injects new life into the series by his vigorous footnotes, which are incidentally his earliest published literary criticism. Since the publication of the *Essay on Man* five years earlier, Pope had been accused of heresy, notably by the learned Swiss divine Jean-Pierre de Crousaz. Crousaz knew no English but was not deterred from printing two sets of remarks, first the *Examen* based on a prose translation and then the *Commentaire* based on the elegant verse translation by the Abbé Du Resnel, with the aid of Voltaire. Pope was vigorously defended by Warburton, and the whole affair was of topical interest. Cave set the learned Miss Elizabeth Carter to work on translating the *Examen*, which she soon completed efficiently, probably by November 1738. Johnson took a little longer, although he was working fast: 'I have written six sheets in a day of translation from the French,' he told Boswell. The Commentary was issued with 1739 on the title-page; but it was withdrawn almost at once, probably because the whole subject suddenly fell flat. Boswell could not find a copy of this rare book and its authorship was established only in this century. It is an odd piece of work: the whole of Du Resnel's version is given, with a word-by-word crib underneath each line, not always very accurate; Johnson adapts Crousaz's dry prose into swelling and mature Johnsonese, freely expanding or contracting his original and chipping in, usually on Pope's side, with sturdy asides, like his comparison of 'Arise, my St. John . . .' and Du Resnel's *Sors de l'enchantement, Milord . . .*: 'the address of one is the exclamation of a freeman, that of the other the murmur of a slave'. Among several themes which he was to develop in his later criticism there is the idea that the French give an exaggerated importance to love:

> Is the mind of man never disordered by any other passion? Is not a wise man sometimes surprized by envy or cowardice, by ambition or resentment? Is all weakness and folly the consequence of love? But it is the general genius of that airy people; debar them from love, and you debar them from poetry. . . . It is evident that it [love] is far from

> operating so powerfully or so universally in the world as it appears to do upon the stage.

Love did not operate powerfully on Johnson at this stage of his career: indeed, he may have been temporarily parted from Tetty. Nor is it likely that he had any other affairs of the heart, although he may well have had some experiences which greatly troubled his conscience in his old age. His true passion was for talk. In pursuit of good conversation he abandoned the prospects of a career and a home, for the taverns and coffee houses where the best talkers were to be found, and if he could not afford such modest resting-places, to wander off into the night through the streets of London, still talking. At this time, and at intervals until the pension came, Johnson was as complete a Bohemian as Dylan Thomas, if not Rimbaud; and his chief companion was the poet Richard Savage. Savage had the kind of paranoid genius that is infinitely rewarding to admirers and exasperating to everyone else: his brilliance and unfulfilled promise are wonderfully described in Johnson's *Life* (1744).

> He lodged as much by Accident as he dined, and passed the Night sometimes in mean Houses, which are set open at Night to any casual Wanderers, sometimes in Cellars among the Riot and Filth of the meanest and most profligate of the Rabble; and sometimes, when he had no Money to support even the Expences of these Receptacles, walked about the Streets until he was weary, and lay down in the Summer upon a Bulk, or in the Winter, with his associates in Poverty, among the Ashes of a Glass-house. . . .
>
> Whoever was acquainted with him, was certain to be solicited for small Sums, which the Frequency of the Request made in Time considerable, and he was therefore quickly shunned by those who were become familiar enough to be trusted with his Necessities. . . .

This is a chapter in Johnson's unfinished autobiography: he was one of the associates in poverty and undoubtedly one of those who kept Savage going with small sums. It explains why Savage chose as a title for his poem *The Wanderer*, and Johnson *The Rambler*; they had both been on the road.

Johnson's interest in London flagged temporarily after he had said good-bye to Savage in July 1739. Leaving Tetty behind, he went off to try again for a post as a schoolmaster. His efforts were again to no avail, and instead of searching around for jobs he spent a lazy six months staying with his friend John Taylor at Ashbourne in Derbyshire; he also visited Lichfield, where the bookshop, run by his mother and his step-daughter, was doing very badly. He was again in pleasant and civilized provincial company. His meeting with Molly Aston, Walmsley's sister-in-law, was one of the events in his life, since he told Mrs Thrale, 'I wonder when any body ever experiences measureless delight: I never did I'm sure except the first Evening I spent Teste a Teste with Molly Aston.' Nevertheless he had to return to Tetty, who had hurt a leg; and he did not return to Lichfield for over twenty years.

He went back to the intermittent grind of the *Gentleman's Magazine*, to the Parliamentary debates and occasional articles. To his Bohemian friends he added the poet William Collins, whose

> appearance was decent and manly; his knowledge considerable, his views extensive, his conversation elegant, and his disposition chearful. By degrees I gained his confidence; and one day was admitted to him when he was immured by a bailiff, that was prowling in the street. On this occasion recourse was had to the booksellers, who, on the credit of a translation of Aristotle's Poeticks, which he engaged to write with a large commentary, advanced as much money as enabled him to escape into the country.

The literary fraternity often suffered from the importunity of creditors; Johnson himself was in trouble over his debts more than once, and was always as generous as he could be to fellow-authors. It must be understood here, although Johnson is too modest to say so, that it was he who got Collins the contract for translating Aristotle, just as he rescued Goldsmith on a later occasion by selling *The Vicar of Wakefield* for him. Johnson at all times gave away his money, when he had any, as well as his time and energy in good offices, with profusion, much to the irritation of his wife. A great many eighteenth-century poets, like good poets in all ages, were careless with their money, getting and spending, cadging and standing treat equally freely. Grub Street has always lived in a happy state of primitive communism; and of this irresponsibility the Great Moralist never showed his disapproval. Indeed his indignation was turned on the commercially minded outsiders who tried to recover their loans, and on the monstrous law which gave them power to imprison their creditors.

In 1743 Richard Savage, the most notorious of petty creditors, died in the sloth and darkness of the Newgate prison of Bristol; and this shocked Johnson into activity. He very rapidly wrote *An Account of the Life of Mr. Richard Savage, Son of the Earl Rivers*, which was published early in 1744. The story of Savage's noble bastardy is a highly romantic one, a fairy-tale of the Male Cinderella with an unhappy ending, and Johnson tells it with great narrative skill. The hero was 'a Man equally distinguished by his Virtue and Vices, and at once remarkable for his Weaknesses and Abilities'; and so Johnson does nothing extenuate nor aught set down in malice. The result is a new kind of biography, which gives an objective picture of the complexities of a most puzzling subject; new at least in English, since it is surpassed by the character-studies of Saint-Simon (which Johnson could not of course have read), although Johnson is superior to Saint-Simon for gentle irony and sympathy. There is a certain amount of rhetoric, and formal balancing of praise and blame in the traditional manner; but in its cool presentation of fantastic or telling details it would serve as the ideal for a modern 'profile'. It is not only a tragi-comedy but a deeply felt and personal tribute; for Savage was his friend and one of his masters in the art of conversation:

> He mingled in cursory Conversation with the same Steadiness of Attention as others apply to a Lecture, and, amidst the Appearance of thoughtless Gayety, lost no new Idea that was started, nor any Hint that could be improved.

These words could be applied to Johnson himself.

About this time Johnson turned his attention to literary criticism, and in the spring of 1745 appeared his *Observations on Macbeth* and his *Proposals* for editing a new edition of Shakespeare. The few brilliant pages of the *Observations* increased his reputation, but he was unable to get support for the edition because of copyright difficulties. Nothing is known of his activities through most of 1745 and the early part of 1746. He may have been suffering from another attack of depression or from increased domestic troubles. But, if anyone wishes to suppose with John Buchan (in his novel *Midwinter*) that Johnson went off to join Prince Charles's army, there is nothing known at present to stop him. Johnson's Jacobitism certainly cooled in later life, but little or nothing is known of his political temperature in 1745. That he should have gone to the North is no more surprising than that several respectable literary figures of today should have gone to the Spanish Civil War in 1936–39. But of course there is not the slightest bit of evidence that he did so.

Although Johnson at thirty-six had little but failure and wasted time behind him, he was known in the literary world for what he was, a man capable of anything. A syndicate of booksellers, who had plans for a profitable enterprise as well as for a public service, asked him to edit a dictionary of the English language, in return for a substantial sum. When nine years of lexicographical drudgery were over, he would be Dictionary Johnson, a household word.

Chapter 3

LONDON; LEXICOGRAPHER

3 LONDON; Lexicographer

1746–1756

It is difficult to form a clear picture of Johnson between the ages of thirty-six and forty-five, as he was engaged on his great work. Nearly all the portraits and recorded conversations or anecdotes come from later periods. One knows of his great height and strength, physical courage, sometimes even violence. It is fairly certain that as at other ages he alternated between slothful melancholy and bursts of concentrated energy, between gaiety in company and intense misery in solitude. Boswell obtained a story, to be dated as 1753, from Reynolds: when Hogarth was visiting the novelist Richardson and discussing politics, 'he perceived a person standing at a window in the room, shaking his head, and rolling himself about in a strange manner. He concluded that he was an idiot, whom his relations had placed under the care of Mr. Richardson, as a very good man.' But the figure stalked forwards and delivered an amazingly eloquent invective against George II. Johnson's strange movements, according to informed medical opinion, were not caused by epilepsy, nor St Vitus' Dance, nor was he a spastic. He suffered rather from multiple tics, involuntary compulsive movements like whistling, shaking his head, rubbing his knee, and rolling from side to side as he walked: most notably, he performed strange ritual actions, as on entering a house or even a room. These tics ceased when he began his wonderful speeches, focusing his mind wholly on the subject: they were therefore of psychic and not physical origin. It is said that such compulsive symptoms are often the result of worry about masturbation, during puberty or later; and such an explanation would seem to fit Johnson. As described by Boswell he seems to have been in a state of high sexual tension throughout his life; and most of all during his *Dictionary* period. Tetty, now abandoned to hypochondria, drink and opium, apparently had banished him from her bed for many years: he philandered with other women, particularly with Mrs Desmoulins, about this time, but with that lady at least his relation remained technically chaste. The subject is uncongenial; but these comments are not meant to imply that Johnson is yet another 'neurotic genius'. The wonder is that he overcame these and so many other disabilities.

Unhappy as he must have been, Johnson was no longer too badly off: the booksellers gave him enough to live on until the *Dictionary* was published. He settled down to the long grind, which began with a massive reading of English literature and works of science: as he read, he marked passages for his six amanuenses to copy on slips. He could afford to pay only a small wage to these assistants, but gave to at least some of them lodgings in his own house: at first in Holborn, and then from 1749 at the famous address in Gough Square. For years on end there were no holidays, and no journeys farther than Hampstead, where Tetty would stay to escape from London's smoke and fogs.

If Johnson's life was static during this period, so was the life of the country. Political affairs were unexciting: after the fall of Walpole in 1742 the country was ruled by the Pelhams, who were inactive in home and foreign policy; there was little intelligent opposition to give an edge to political life. The War of the Austrian Succession was virtually over in 1747, and England was at peace until the Seven Years War. Public affairs vexed no man. Imports and exports rose slowly, but England was still a country of traders and domestic producers. With the passing of the Act of 1751 the great social evil of gin-drinking was somewhat diminished: although the death-rate fell slightly, there was no great improvement in public health. A succession of good harvests kept the people happy. In literary life as well as political there was a dull interregnum. Pope had died in 1744, Swift the year after; the only notable works of literature to appear were *Clarissa*, *Tom Jones*, and *An Elegy written in a Country Church-*

yard; the leading figure in journalism was probably Smollett. Pope's prophecy about the spread of Dullness seemed to have come true in the fields of philosophy and science also: the deist controversy died away, while David Hume was still little known. As in our own mid-century, there was little to compare with the excitements of the 'twenties and 'thirties.

A man's fortieth birthday is a melancholy event, if he has achieved little by then. Perhaps to mark the occasion, Johnson in 1749 wrote at his usual great speed, *The Vanity of Human Wishes*, his greatest triumph in poetry and the noblest expression of his melancholy. Like Gray's *Elegy*, the *Vanity* is a poem about frustration: following Juvenal, Johnson proves by examples from history that it is useless to pray for personal endowments, such as wealth, political power, learning, military prowess, long life, or beauty. Each brings its own retribution or negation, and so the Christian Stoic must ask God only 'for a Healthy Mind, Obedient Passions and a Will resign'd'. Of the fallacious blessings he lists, Johnson was to possess only two: learning, and in some measure long life. The latter he feared and with justice, since he thought that his physical and mental infirmities might turn him into a Struldbrug, or, worse, into a dismal replica of the Struldbrug's creator. Johnson saw something of Swift in himself, the demonic energy, the fantastic imagination, the possibility of mania; nearly all his references to Swift in conversation or writing show an aggressive hostility that comes from fear; and this gives his final couplet on old age its peculiar tremor of dread:

> *From* Marlb'rough's *Eyes the Streams of Dotage flow,*
> *And* Swift *expires a Driv'ler and a Show.*

The poem gains some of its strength from its vision of history. 'Let Hist'ry tell', Johnson says, its sad truths, to point a moral and adorn a tale. This is the medieval view of history, not as a rational explanation of growth and change, but as a tragic catalogue of the splendours and follies of the great: 'They mount, they shine, evaporate, and fall.' But he also takes the heroic view of history: his examples show a baroque grandeur rather than a medieval gloom. From 'the steady Romans' who 'shook the world' to 'the bold Bavarian' who 'Tries the dread Summit of *Cesarean* Pow'r', all are illumined by the ceremonious latinity of Johnson's diction and the solemn beat of the verse.

But even here Johnson cannot help talking for victory. Take the wonderful passage where he is talking of the one gift of fortune that was not denied to him:

When first the College Rolls receive his Name,
The young Enthusiast quits his Ease for Fame;
Resistless burns the Fever of Renown,
Caught from the strong Contagion of the Gown;
O'er Bodley'*s Dome his future Labours spread,*
And Bacon'*s Mansion trembles o'er his Head;*
Are these thy Views? proceed, illustrious Youth,
And Virtue guard thee to the Throne of Truth,
Yet should thy Soul indulge the gen'rous Heat,
Till captive Science yields her last Retreat;
Should Reason guide thee with her brightest Ray,
And pour on misty Doubt resistless Day;
Should no false Kindness lure to loose Delight,
Nor Praise relax, nor Difficulty fright;
Should tempting Novelty thy Cell refrain,
And Sloth's bland Opiates shed their Fumes in vain;
Should Beauty blunt on Fops her fatal Dart,
Nor claim the Triumph of a letter'd Heart;
Should no Disease thy torpid Veins invade,
Nor Melancholy's Phantoms haunt thy Shade;
Yet hope not Life from Grief or Danger free,
Nor think the Doom of Man revers'd for thee:
Deign on the passing World to turn thine Eyes,
And pause awhile from Learning to be wise;
There mark what Ills the Scholar's Life assail,
Toil, Envy, Want, the Garret, and the Jail.

In his revised version, Johnson, thinking of Lord Chesterfield, altered 'Garret' to 'Patron', heightening the serio-comic catalogue of miseries. That this magnificent rhetoric contains absurd exaggerations Johnson would not have denied: not all these assail even the most wretched academic. In the writing of satire, as of lapidary inscriptions, a man is not upon oath. We are not meant to take this as the considered view of Samuel Johnson, but rather as those of a malcontent persona, dressed in Juvenal's singing robes or peering from Diogenes' tub. The passage is full of deliciously elaborate periphrasis, as in the descriptions of idleness and love (which are of course very real enemies of scholarship). The final effect here and in some other parts of the poem is one of burlesque, almost of mock heroic, like the tremendous ending of the *Dunciad*. Johnson, like Pope, mistrusted his poetic genius unless it was used to moralistic ends, and yet often refused to present his moral truths unless they were dressed in wit or absurdity. This argues a lack of confidence in poetry—yet no one did any better than *The Vanity of Human Wishes* until Wordsworth.

The poem brought Johnson fame if little profit; and by now Garrick was well enough established in the theatre to risk putting on a play by his brilliant friend. This was a revised version of the tragedy *Irene*, which Johnson had been carrying in his pocket for a dozen years. It was not a success and has not survived as literature; and Boswell has told us all we need to know about this event. Johnson like all writers was irritated by the producer's changes in the script: 'the fellow wants to make Mahomet run mad, that he may have an opportunity of tossing his hands and kicking his heels'. Further changes had to be made after the first night, because of 'the conclusion, when Mrs. Pritchard, playing the heroine, was to be strangled upon the stage, and had to speak two lines with the bow-string round her neck. The audience cried out *Murder! Murder!*' For the first night, Johnson for once altered his usual style of dress, appearing 'behind the scenes, and even in one of the side boxes, in a scarlet waistcoat, with rich gold lace, and a gold-laced hat'; but when asked how he felt about the play's failure, he replied, 'Like the Monument'. So ended Johnson's first and only contact with the theatre, apart from writing prologues; he even told Garrick, according to Hume, that he would never return to the green-room, 'for the silk stocking and white bosoms of your actresses excite my amorous propensities' (the original is franker).

As a break from the routine of dictionary-making, and to make a little extra money, Johnson now undertook a bi-weekly essay in the well-established tradition of the *Spectator*. The *Rambler* ran from March 1750 until just before Tetty's death in March 1752. He wrote each essay at great speed, often at the last minute with the compositor's boy standing at his elbow, although the majestic and polished sentences show no trace of haste. The original essays sold only moderately well, but the collected reprints did rather better, establishing Johnson as a teacher of wisdom. Few have ever shared Boswell's profound veneration of this work, and even to read it through is now a task for professional scholars only. Nothing dates faster than minor moralistic writing; only that which offers either a highly logical exposition or a burning spiritual vision is tolerable after a generation. Yet every age loves its preachers, as ours loves the psychologists, educationalists, and literary critics who tell us how to live. The eighteenth century was an age of sermons, as one can see from a glance at any old library. There were thousands of clerical sermons (and Johnson, as we shall see, wrote many of these for his friends in Holy Orders), rationally explaining the benefits of good conduct; and almost as many lay sermons, in the periodical essays which followed strictly the tradition laid down by Addison. Addison by his immense prestige destroyed the 'familiar' essay of Montaigne, which did not appear again until the early nineteenth century with Hazlitt and Lamb. Instead of tracing the contours of a reflective mind, the eighteenth-century essayists repeat the prescribed pattern of homily, Theophrastian 'Character', imaginary letter, and non-academic literary criticism, all aimed at the improvement of taste and manners, or the correction of social follies that were beneath the dignity of the pulpit to mention. Johnson's *Rambler* essays fit precisely into the Addisonian mould, but lack Addison's sophistication and spontaneous gaiety. They contain some of the finest sentences and paragraphs in which Johnson's wisdom is enshrined, but they are disappointing when read complete. In the interests of reminding the public of the great truths of morality, the argument is usually kept at a level which does not call forth Johnson's full intellectual powers; thus they lack the fire and excitement that the greatest ethical writing, from Plato to Kierkegaard, can offer us. As social comment, the essays are too abstract, too far removed from the life of London seething around their author: only in the noble essays on the criminal law does he make anything of an urgent problem.

The style of the *Rambler*, forbidding on first sight, is fascinating to analyse. The rhetoric, 'Johnsonese' at its most typical, with the long, balanced sentences and rolling swell, is partly modelled on the cadences of Sir Thomas Browne and Cicero. The polysyllabic vocabulary, on the other hand, has its origin in something other than Johnson's literary studies. As Professor W. K. Wimsatt has shown in *Philosophic Words* (1948), many of the long words are technical, drawn from the immense amount of scientific books Johnson had just been searching through to illustrate his dictionary; and he was the first to use many of these words in a transferred sense, inventing new metaphors which greatly extended the scope of the English language. Johnson did this deliberately: 'I have familiarized the Terms of Philosophy (i.e. Natural Science) by applying them to known Objects and popular Ideas', he wrote in the last essay. In ordinary prose today we should not hesitate to use such words as 'aberration, absorb, accelerate, amalgamate, attraction, volatile, volubility, vulnerable' (to quote from Wimsatt's list) in order to describe everyday experiences; we are likely to forget that such words were originally scientific jargon. In rescuing many of these words from the specialists and giving them to literature, Johnson showed imaginative daring and tact. Sometimes indeed he failed ludicrously: 'when from the adscititious Happiness all the Deductions have been made, by Fear and Accident, there will remain nothing equiponderant to the Security of Truth' (No. 20) is an elephantine sentence, but 'the Incidents which give Excellence to Biography are of a volatile and evanescent Kind' (No. 60) shows a picturesque and telling use of the 'language of Chymistry'.

The quotations in the *Dictionary* show how widely and carefully Johnson had read in the seventeenth-century scientists, from Bacon to Newton, and especially in those of the great age of the Royal Society, which had ended before his birth, in Boyle, Glanvill, and Ray. It is certain that he had an excellent understanding of what he read; for Johnson the gap between the 'Two Cultures', between the humanities and the sciences, hardly existed. Like Bacon, he could have taken all knowledge as his province, except in the one respect of mathematics. Johnson was fond of arithmetic, and was always making calculations, but almost certainly he lacked the power to grasp the advances made in the seventeenth century, from Napier's logarithms to the calculus of Newton and Leibnitz, stopping at the barrier that ever since has shut off so many intelligent people from natural science. Mathematics apart, Johnson's grasp was firm. He knew much of what there was to know about medicine: he confidently prescribed drugs for himself and in his last illness kept a detailed and technical journal of his symptoms. He kept the orange peel from the punch-bowl to make into a laxative; he wrote the life of the Dutch physician Boerhaave; and he talked often and intelligently about his own indifferent health. Chemistry was perhaps his favourite: he performed experiments in his London garret and we shall see him doing so on a more ambitious scale with Mrs Thrale at Streatham. He was too short-sighted for botany or zoology, but he carefully incorporated the best authorities on these subjects in the *Dictionary*.

After the spectacular advances of the later seventeenth century, science now appeared to be marking time. The Royal Society had lost much of its prestige, even before Swift satirized it in *Gulliver's Travels*, while no contemporary scientist or mathematician enjoyed the glory of Newton. Useful work, however, was done by Halley and Bradley in astronomy, and by Boerhaave in chemistry; and there was a steady advance in pure mathematics. In zoology Buffon's was the most famous name, and the essential work of classifying the species had been begun by Carl Linnaeus in the 'thirties. With most of this work Johnson appeared to be familiar; the next major steps, as by Herschel in astronomy and by Cavendish and Priestley in chemistry, were made only towards the end of his life.

If the mid-eighteenth century was not a great period for pure science, it was very much the age of technology. Johnson had been born in the Age of Steam, since in 1708 Thomas Newcomen had invented the atmospheric engine, before long to be widely used for pumping mines; James Watt invented the steam engine proper in 1764. This was also the beginning of the new Iron Age, since from about 1709 the new coke smelting process had been developing slowly. Kay's flying shuttle (1733), Hargreave's spinning jenny (1767), Roebuck's process for making sulphuric acid (1746), the improved marine chronometers—these are examples of the creative energy of the English inventors, who preceded the Industrial Revolution and made it possible. Johnson was fascinated by the progress of technology and industry, and unusually well-informed. Richard Arkwright, the great inventor, pronounced Johnson to be the only person who, on a first view, understood both the principle and powers of the most complicated pieces of machinery. He understood his father's tannery and Henry Thrale's brewery equally well. He belonged to the Society of Arts and Manufactures, one of the

7 St Clement Danes, where Johnson worshipped, and the Strand, in 1753
From a print by J. Maurer

A

DICTIONARY

OF THE

ENGLISH LANGUAGE:

IN WHICH

The WORDS are deduced from their ORIGINALS,

AND

ILLUSTRATED in their DIFFERENT SIGNIFICATIONS

BY

EXAMPLES from the beſt WRITERS.

TO WHICH ARE PREFIXED,

A HISTORY of the LANGUAGE,

AND

AN ENGLISH GRAMMAR.

BY SAMUEL JOHNSON, A.M.

IN TWO VOLUMES.

VOL. I.

Cum tabulis animum cenſoris ſumet honeſti;
Audebit quæcunque parum ſplendoris habebunt,
Et ſine pondere erunt, et honore indigna ferentur.
Verba movere loco; quamvis invita recedant,
Et verſentur adhuc intra penetralia Veſtæ:
Obſcurata diu populo bonus eruet, atque
Proferet in lucem ſpecioſa vocabula rerum,
Quæ priſcis memorata Catonibus atque Cethegis,
Nunc ſitus informis premit et deſerta vetuſtas. HOR.

LONDON,
Printed by W. STRAHAN,
For J. and P. KNAPTON; T. and T. LONGMAN; C. HITCH and L. HAWES;
A. MILLAR; and R. and J. DODSLEY.
MDCCLV.

8 The title-page of the first edition of the *Dictionary* (1755)

associations formed to encourage technical advance in industry, and wrote prefaces to such works as Rolt's *Dictionary of Trade and Commerce* (1756), and Payne's *New Tables of Interest* (1758), the titles of which show his practical bias. In his benevolent interest in applied science, industrial technique, and expanding trade, and in his sane belief in progress, Johnson was a man of his age.

In 1752 Johnson had cares besides writing the *Rambler* and reading science: Tetty died in March, after some years of poor health. It is impossible to say how Johnson felt. In later years he venerated her memory and wrote pathetically about her in his private journals; while Boswell, to spite Hawkins, piously fostered the opinion that it had been a happy marriage. Johnson's other acquaintances thought differently, and Mrs Thrale quotes the two most reliable witnesses: 'Garrick says the Woman was a little painted Poppet; full of Affectation and rural Airs of Elegance; old Levett says She was always drunk & reading Romances in her Bed, where She killed herself by taking Opium.' I share Clifford's view that Johnson's irrational feelings of guilt made him romanticize his dead wife: the more melancholy he became, the more he would unjustly blame himself for any unhappiness that had arisen between them. It is certain that in a year he was thinking of re-marriage, and writing in his journal: 'As I purpose to try on Monday to seek a new wife without any derogation from dear Tettys memory I purpose at sacrament in the morning to take my leave of Tetty in a solemn commendation of her soul to God.' It is not known whom he intended to ask, but Johnson had quite a wide circle of woman friends to choose from: despite his appearance and manners he was always attractive to women. Whatever happened in 1753 he soon settled down to confirmed celibacy, a way of life thus described in *Rasselas*:

> To live without feeling or exciting sympathy, to be fortunate without adding to the felicity of others, or afflicted without tasting the balm of pity, is a state more gloomy than solitude: it is not retreat but exclusion from mankind. Marriage has many pains, but celibacy has no pleasures.

By the end of 1752 Johnson had started writing essays again, this time for a periodical called *The Adventurer*, to which, however, he contributed only about thirty essays in a year and a half. The final stages of preparing the *Dictionary* called for his concentrated attention. He was behind his schedule at the beginning of 1753 but finished in a strong burst of work. It now became generally known that he was actually fulfilling the ambitious and masterly *Plan of a Dictionary of the English Language*, which he had published in 1747, 'Addressed to the Right Honourable Philip Dormer, Earl of Chesterfield, One of His Majesty's Principal Secretaries of State'. This admirable man, as statesmanlike as he was literate, had agreed to become Johnson's patron, by accepting the dedication and giving him ten pounds, which was as much as the publishers had given him for *London*. He then presumably forgot all about the matter, as he well might, if Johnson had done nothing to remind him of the work in progress. But even before the *Dictionary* was published, probably looking at proof sheets sent to him by the anxious publishers, Chesterfield tried to make amends by writing two handsome articles in the *World*. Johnson's reply, in a semi-public and beautifully written letter, is partly an outbreak of his 'mad and violent' temperament, an explosion of bloody-mindedness, and partly a symbolical repudiation of the feudal ties between noble lord and dependent. He was now his own man, financially supported by the public and about to receive universal recognition as the Great Cham of scholarship.

> Is not a Patron, My Lord, one who looks with unconcern on a Man struggling for Life in the Water and when he has reached ground encumbers him with help. The notice which you have been pleased to take of my Labours, had it been early, had been kind; but it has been delayed till I am indifferent and cannot enjoy it, till I am solitary and cannot impart it, till I am known and do not want it.

Just before the Chesterfield incident Johnson had taken his first trip for many years: he spent five weeks in Oxford, his first return to his university. Thanks to the good offices of his friend the poet Thomas Warton, the Heads of Houses and Convocation in February 1755 conferred on him the degree of Master of Arts, in time for this distinction to appear on the title-page of the *Dictionary*. (This would now be called an honorary degree, of M.A.; he was not yet Doctor Johnson.) The *Dictionary* was published on 15th April.

The *Dictionary* established Johnson as one of the Makers of England. It was not the first of its kind, nor did it contain the largest number of words; but because of its literary qualities, its readability and clarity, it held a peculiar authority over all who wrote English for more than a century. Johnson combined several things in his two large folios: a lexicon of the language, with an explanation of each word in its various senses; a guide to correct usage; and a set of illustrations from the best writers from the Elizabethans to himself. In addition, it was a kind of encyclopaedia, with technical articles assembled, not very systematically, from other works of reference; and, of least importance, it gave etymologies which were often wrong. Its normative function was the most significant. By gaining acceptance as a legislator of standard meanings, it gave its users confidence in the stability of the language, and had a social effect comparable with the introduction of standard weights and measures, or the invention of the thermometer scale. It thus helped to 'purify the dialect of the tribe' and to form the admirable lingua franca used by English (and American) statesmen, business men, sailors, and poets until well into the nineteenth century.

Johnson knew that language cannot be permanently fixed, but undergoes continual growth and change. Although it was not his purpose to make an historical dictionary, like the modern *Oxford English Dictionary*, he gave such an ordered wealth of illustrations from two hundred years of literature that his readers could not fail to gain some insight into the history of the language. It was, however, his original intention to provide a kind of anthology of fine writing, by illustrating the words with 'flowers of speech' picked from the greatest writers. He had to shorten this part (noticeably after the letter A) because of reasons of space; but enough is left to convince a reader that good English is the English of Bacon and Shakespeare. Where Johnson has remained supreme among lexicographers, as Wimsatt has pointed out,[1] is in his understanding of metaphor, of the relations between the primary and transferred senses of words; and in that he shows a poet's understanding. The *Dictionary* prevailed because it was a personal literary creation, as is shown not only in the comic definitions (oats, Excise, Whig,

[1] 'Johnson's Dictionary' in *New Light on Dr. Johnson*, 1959.

Grub Street)[1] but in the verve and lucidity of hundreds of articles.

Finally, in making the *Dictionary* Johnson made himself. From years of immense reading of primary sources, most of them now firmly committed to his prodigious memory, he emerged as the undisputed arbiter, fit and ready to govern the kingdom of letters.

[1] 'The name of a street in London, much inhabited by writers of small histories, dictionaries, and temporary poems; whence any mean production is called *Grub-street*.'

9 *From an engraving by Finden*

Chapter 4

THE MORALIST

4 THE MORALIST

1756–1762

When the *Dictionary* had been published and acclaimed, Johnson found himself famous, but hardly better off. He had spent all the money received from the publishers, and there were no royalties to come in. Early in 1756 he was even arrested for a debt of £5 18*s*. and had to be rescued by the novelist Richardson. For the next six years life was always difficult. He had his large and miscellaneous 'family' to support: the blind Mrs Williams, the widowed Mrs Desmoulins (daughter of his Lichfield godfather), the quack doctor Levett, as well as his Negro servant Frank Barber. Various other hangers-on lived in his house from time to time; at a later date these included Poll Carmichael, described by Mrs Thrale as a pauper 'Scotch Wench' and of whom Johnson said to Fanny Burney: 'Poll is a stupid slut; I had some hopes of her at first; but when I talked to her tightly and closely, I could make nothing of her; she was wiggle-waggle, and I could never persuade her to be categorical.' The 'family' was often quarrelsome and needed Johnson's services as peace-maker; and his time and money were also spent in keeping open house to distressed authors and bankrupt booksellers, the casualties of literature. In prosperity or adversity his charity was unstinted. It extended to the beggars he passed in the streets, whose appeals he could never resist. He was just as noted for his kindness to children and to animals. When he went in person to buy the moderate luxury of oysters for his cat Hodge, this was to spare the feelings of Frank, who might have resented doing such menial service. With his instinct to put himself in the place of any other creature—an instinct which guided all his moral comment—he was even tender of Hodge's feelings. To Boswell's praise he replied, 'Why yes, Sir, but I have had cats whom I liked better than this'; and then as if perceiving Hodge to be out of countenance, adding, 'but he is a very fine cat, a very fine cat indeed.'

In a man's late forties he no longer enjoys the pleasures of Bohemianism, and Johnson aspired to domesticity and a good table. But in 1759 because of poverty the 'family' had to be partially dispersed: the house in Gough Square was given up and Mrs Williams sent to lodgings; Johnson took rooms in Gray's Inn, then occupied the first floor of Inner Temple Lane No. 1, where Arthur Murphy found him living in 'poverty, total idleness, and the pride of literature'. His poverty was aggravated by his idleness. He had to find some large-scale undertaking, comparable with the *Dictionary*, and naturally turned to the editing of Shakespeare, which he had been thinking about since he published 'Observations' on *Macbeth* and 'Proposals' for an edition in 1745. In 1756 his new 'Proposals' were taken up eagerly by the publisher Tonson, and his contract for a subscription edition would have been a profitable one, if he had been able to complete the work promptly. But what was originally planned to take two years eventually took nine, and one may suspect that most of the work was done in the last of these years, long after the publisher's advance had been spent. Meanwhile Johnson, the despair of his friends and admirers, fell back on journalism for a precarious living. Much of this consisted of book-reviewing for the *Literary Magazine* during 1756–57, the best of which was his long study of Soame Jenyns's *Free Enquiry*. From 1758 to 1760 he returned to essay-writing, with a series appropriately called 'The Idler' in the *Universal Chronicle*. In 1759, in order to pay for his mother's funeral, he wrote *Rasselas*, which is nearly as long as this book, in the evenings of one week, sending it off to the printer in sections, without revising. There are a number of prefaces and dedications, written for other authors with his usual generosity; and that, until the Pension made it unnecessary to earn a living, was all.

Three of the works of this period would by themselves earn Johnson his place in English literature. The review of *A Free Inquiry*

10 Johnson in 1756
From the painting by Sir Joshua Reynolds

11 Boswell and Johnson
From a drawing attributed to Samuel Collings

12 Boswell
From a pencil sketch by Sir Thomas Lawrence

into the Nature and Origin of Evil is a masterpiece of irony, and a noble statement of Johnson's humanism. Soame Jenyns's is one of several eighteenth-century theodicies that try to explain human suffering by the Great Chain of Being. He assumes that every Platonic Idea has a valid claim to existence; that a universe which left a single Idea unrealized would be incomplete; and that there is a hierarchy of actualized Ideas from highest to lowest. Leibnitz summarized the principle by saying that God 'preferred that the imperfect should exist rather than nothing', Pope more simply by 'Whatever is, is right'. The theory conveniently explains the parts of nature that are red in tooth and claw, the polio virus and the H-bomb, since, if such embarrassing things did not exist, there would be links missing in the chain. Man is himself only another link in the chain, and according to Jenyns there may well be spiritual beings somewhere above us in the scale of creation, 'who may deceive, torment or destroy us, for the ends, only, of their own pleasure or utility'. The imperfections or sufferings of one part of the chain benefit the other parts, hence the necessity of pain and poverty: 'the sufferings of individuals are absolutely necessary to general happiness'. This monstrous optimism was attacked by Johnson as mordantly as by Voltaire:

> Many of the books which now crowd the world, may justly be suspected to be written for the sake of some invisible order of beings, for surely they are of no use to any of the corporeal inhabitants of the world. . . . The only end of writing is to enable the readers better to enjoy life, or better to endure it; and how will either of those be put into our power, by him who tells us, that we are puppets, of which some creature, not much wiser than ourselves, manages the wires. That a set of beings, unseen and unheard, are hovering about us, trying experiments upon our sensibility, putting us in agonies to see our limbs quiver; torturing us to madness, that they may laugh at our vagaries; sometimes obstructing the bile, that they may see how a man looks when he is yellow; sometimes breaking a traveller's bones to try how he will get home; sometimes wasting a man to a skeleton, and sometimes killing him fat for the greater elegance of his hide.

The irony, especially of the last sentence, is Swiftian: Johnson uses Swift's device of presenting concrete and brutal images in opposition to the smug abstractions he is attacking. Against Jenyns's generalities about the cosmological necessity for poverty, Johnson places his realistic understanding of other men's sufferings and his own experience. Johnson's greatness as a moralist and a man comes out in the following passage: he has no formal system to offer in place of the theodicies, but his vision of the human situation is a true one.

> The milder degrees of poverty are, sometimes, supported by hope; but the more severe often sink down in motionless dependence. Life must be seen before it can be known. This author and Pope perhaps never saw the miseries which they imagine thus easy to be borne. The poor, indeed, are insensible of many little vexations, which sometimes imbitter the possessions, and pollute the enjoyments of the rich. They are not pained by casual incivility, or mortified by the mutilation of a compliment; but this happiness is like that of a malefactor, who ceases to feel the cords that bind him, when the pincers are tearing his flesh. . . .

When Johnson published the *Idler* essays in a collected edition, he added one called 'On the Bravery of the Common English Soldiers'; inspired by the victories of the Seven Years War, it is a warm tribute to the people from which he sprang. At the same time it shows keen observation of society; Johnson had learned from the great free-thinker Mandeville, whose *Fable of the Bees* (1724), a pioneer essay in sociology, he said 'opened my views into real life very much'. In attributing the English soldier's courage to the 'dissolution of dependance', that is to the breaking up of traditional patriarchal ties, rather than to love of liberty or patriotism, he is as realistic and empirical as ever. His attitude to the turbulent mob, who threw mud at the rich and beat up foreigners on sight, shows sympathy without cant.

> There are some, perhaps, who would imagine, that every Englishman fights better than the subjects of absolute governments, because he has more to defend. But what has the English more than the French soldier? Property they are both commonly without. Liberty is, to the lowest rank of every nation, little more than the choice of working or starving; and this choice is, I suppose, equally allowed in every country. The English soldier seldom has his head very full of the constitution; nor has there been, for more than a century, any war that put the property or liberty of a single Englishman in danger.
>
> Whence, then, is the courage of the English vulgar? It proceeds, in my opinion, from that dissolution of dependance, which obliges every man to regard his own character. . . . Every man that crowds our streets is a man of honour, disdainful of obligation, impatient of reproach, and

> desirous of extending his reputation among those of his own rank; and as courage is in most frequent use, the fame of courage is most easily pursued. . . . They who complain, in peace, of the insolence of the populace, must remember, that their insolence in peace is bravery in war.

The third great work of the 'fifties is of course *Rasselas*. It is of great interest to any biographer; since it was written very quickly and without effort, it accidentally reveals much of the state of Johnson's mind at this time. There is, for example, a moving passage in Chapter 45, about the astronomer who suffered from the delusion that he could control the weather and make the rain fall at the right time. 'If I am accidentally left alone for a few hours, said he, my inveterate persuasion rushes upon my soul, and my thoughts are chained down by some irresistible violence.' His sufferings are relieved by conversation, just as Johnson's were; but irrational feelings of guilt are always ready to return: 'I am sometimes afraid lest I indulge my guilt by criminal negligence, and voluntarily forget the great charge with which I am intrusted.' Imlac's wise comment shows that Johnson understood his own unhappy condition, if he could do little about it.

> No disease of the imagination . . . is so difficult of cure, as that which is complicated by the dread of guilt: fancy and conscience then act interchangeably upon us, and so often shift their places, that the illusions of one are not distinguished from the dictates of the other.

This 'dangerous prevalence of the imagination' made Johnson fear his own poetic genius: that way madness lay. Potentially a great poet, he deliberately rejected the gifts of imagination which the Muses, daughters of memory, had handed to him. Fearing all his life that madness, to which great wit is near allied, was pressing on him, he chose to abandon the supreme glory of poetry.

Rasselas begins as an exercise, using the fashionable conventions of oriental romance and picaresque; the style is witty and relatively light. On a flimsy framework Johnson spun a web of short essays, on a variety of topics: literary criticism, illusion and reality, a meditation on the pyramids ('all is vanity'), the art of living, and above all on boredom. The prince and princess escape from the Happy Valley of Abyssinia because they are bored, and guided by the literary moralist Imlac explore the busy world outside. Are the

Europeans less bored, because of their science and technology? 'The Europeans, answered Imlac, are less unhappy than we, but they are not happy. Human life is everywhere a state in which much is to be endured, and little to be enjoyed.' The philosophers have little to tell them. In Cairo the professor who lectures on Stoicism is no better able to bear the loss of a child than anyone else. They try the pastoral life, but the shepherds are boorish and disgusting; the Golden Age of the poets is a fiction. A hermit finds solitude intolerable and is about to return to 'the conversation of the good'. Another philosopher tells them to 'live according to nature', but this proves to be mere word-spinning. The rich turn out to be miserable, the poor neither happy nor virtuous; the old man finds his life tedious and useless. At 'the conclusion in which nothing is concluded' they decide to return to Abyssinia, the princess 'to found a college of learned women' and the others to make the best of things.

There are many echoes of the theme of the *Vanity of Human Wishes*, but they are ironic and half-comic echoes. Johnson refuses to adorn the subject of disillusionment with tragic rhetoric; but instead he makes a serious study, almost the first in literature, of that scourge of modern man—*taedium vitae*. It is not quite the first, since it had been discussed in Burton's *Anatomy of Melancholy*, Johnson's favourite book, indeed the only one that made him get out of his bed early to read. *Rasselas* shows us a world in which all are bored, either because like the poor they are imprisoned in their occupations, or because they are egoists, imprisoned in their solitary illusions, like the hermit and the astronomer in their monomania. This was how Johnson heard the still, sad music of humanity. His remedy is expounded with wit and charm: it is a moral duty tokeep boredom at bay, by travel, by studying the arts and sciences, and above all by the social arts of conversation and practical charity. It is an unromantic conclusion, but an adequate justification of Johnson's own way of life. *Rasselas* breathes the charity and sympathy that Johnson tried to inspire in his fellow-men.

At this time Johnson's sole means of escape from sloth, melancholy and the fear of insanity lay in conversation. He might have said with Coleridge, 'The stimulus of conversation suspends the terror that haunts my mind.' He had many friends, not perhaps as extraordinary as Savage or Psalmanazar, nor as gifted as some members of the Club, but Johnson was too shrewd a judge of men to surround himself with knaves or bores. There was Bennet Langton, a Greek scholar, and Topham Beauclerk, a well-bred connoisseur, both twenty years younger than Johnson and lively companions. Above all there was Arthur Murphy, a talented Irish lawyer turned playwright, of about the same age. His conversation, wrote Mrs Thrale (to whom Murphy introduced Johnson), was 'so happily made up of Narration & native good Sense, of Fact & Sentiment, that it is impossible to imagine a more agreeable Man'. If Johnson had died before meeting Boswell and Mrs Thrale, we should still have received a fair notion of his life and talk from Murphy; from Joshua Reynolds, his most distinguished friend of the period; and from Boswell's arch-enemy, Sir John Hawkins.

Johnson's conversation with these men must have been as splendid as when Boswell recorded it, turning as ever on the great topics of books and public affairs. The literary scene was, however, hardly more exciting than in the 'forties. Gray published little except his *Odes*; Collins died insane in 1759. Smollett was a force in journalism, but his novels did not approach the greatness of Richardson or Fielding. Sterne was to revive the spirit of the Queen Anne wits: the aged Lord Bathurst told him he had enjoyed nothing else since the death of his friend Pope, but Johnson dismissed this new star as a trifler, saying perversely a few years later, 'Tristram Shandy did not last'. In philosophy, despite the greatness of Hume, the initiative had passed to France, where the encyclopaedists were hard at work. Voltaire published *Candide* in the same year as *Rasselas*, Rousseau the *Contrat Social* three years later—Johnson cordially detested both. The period saw the rise of Edinburgh as a second capital of the arts and sciences, presided over by Hume, John Home, and Lord Elibank; but the glory of Scotland was to Johnson a matter of indifference.

In politics he took less interest than he was to show in the days of Henry Thrale. He made little comment on the rise of Pitt, and the excitements of the Seven Years War, except briefly on the fate of Admiral Byng. The *Annus Mirabilis*, 1759, left Johnson unenthusiastic, except about the courage of the troops. To the consequent expansion of the Empire he gave no warmer welcome than did anyone else, save the merchants who backed Pitt. Home politics were quiet, before the turmoils of the 'sixties: the harvests were nearly all good, trade flourished and despite the war there was modest prosperity. The accession of George III in 1760 was not a decisive moment for the nation, but it was perhaps so for Johnson. It is certain that his Jacobitism had cooled greatly by this time; and his attitude to the Hanoverians changed further when he discovered that the new King was, in some sense of the word, a Tory.

To one subject Johnson was never indifferent: religion. To this time belong many of the 'Prayers and Meditations' that he wrote down in his private journal. No one has ever doubted that he was a deeply religious man, but since the word 'religious' covers a wide range of human activities and feelings, his position needs to be examined with some care. In the first place, Johnson was a rationalist by temperament, whose empirical bent had been strengthened by his scientific studies. When Boswell asked him 'Has any man the same conviction of the truth of Religion that he has in the common affairs of Life?' he answered 'No, Sir.'—a passage which Boswell omitted from the *Life*. From his reading of the seventeenth-century scientists Johnson took two cardinals of his religion: 'physico-theology' and an interest in psychical research. The early members of the Royal Society had been sincerely pious men, and elaborated the argument from design to prove the existence of God: only a Great Artificer could have formed the wonderful universe revealed by science. Johnson quotes at length from these authors in the *Dictionary* and for him as for most of his contemporaries physico-theology was a comforting stand-by. The Royal Society, in order to refute the materialism of Hobbes, had also encouraged the investigation of ghosts and other examples of 'spirit'. Johnson's interest in the psychic is shown by his research into the Cock Lane Ghost (a fraudulent poltergeist in 1762) and into the 'second sight' of the Hebrideans. He passed his life in a quest for certainty about the supernatural, a certainty which he did not claim to have reached. He never enjoyed anything approaching mystical illumination, or even the spiritual comforts of religion. About one thing only was he certain: the likelihood of his own damnation. This was a literal belief: when Adams asked 'What do you mean by damned?' he replied 'passionately and loudly, "Sent to Hell, Sir, and punished everlastingly".' He thought of himself as no uncommon sinner, and his sins as more than Sloth or Greed. The 'Prayers and Meditations', extremely touching to read in the manuscripts of Pembroke College, Oxford, are sometimes embarrassing in cold print, but that written on Easter Eve 1757 is made less so by the formal beauty of the phrasing.

> Almighty God, heavenly Father, who desirest not the death of a sinner, look down with mercy upon me depraved with vain imaginations, and entangled in long habits of Sin. Grant me that grace without which I can neither will nor do what is acceptable to thee. Pardon my sins, remove the impediments that hinder my obedience. Enable me to shake off Sloth, and to redeem the time mispent in idleness and Sin by a diligent application of the days yet remaining to the duties which thy Providence shall allot me. O God grant me thy Holy Spirit that I may repent and amend my life, grant me contrition, grant me resolution for the sake of Jesus Christ, to whose covenant I now implore admission, of the benefits of whose death I implore participation; for his sake have mercy on me O God; for his sake, O God, pardon and receive me. Amen.

Although he was well read in the Fathers and modern Protestant divines, Johnson did not care to pursue speculative theology beyond the argument from design. The sermons he generously wrote for many clergymen of his acquaintance, where they can be traced, are rational exhortations to duty and righteousness, not very different in content from his moral essays, and in this he followed the standard practice of the age.

Johnson has been accurately described as a pious rather than a devout man. If piety means attachment to the outward forms of religion and loyalty to the Church, for the sake of peace and morality, there was no more fervent advocate of this virtue. Whatever his private beliefs or experience, he was first and foremost a churchman; and to be a churchman meant to defend the political claims and rights of the Established Church of England. In Johnson's Toryism, state and ecclesiastical politics were closely bound together, as they had been in the England of his childhood. For example, one of his first remarks that Boswell heard reported (from Hume) was that he 'would stand before a battery of cannon, to restore the Convocation to its full powers'. Convocation had been suppressed since 1717, the year of the Bangorian Controversy: the turbulent Lower House, representing the Tory and Jacobite country clergy, raised an outcry against the Whig and Erastian Bishops of the Upper House, on the essentially political issue of the Church's subordination to the State. The fact that this issue was dead by the mid-century made little difference to Johnson: he remained loyal to the High Church party of the days of Queen Anne and Dr Sacheverell. In Johnson's England little but a political meaning could be attached to the word 'High'. Since the Non-Jurors there had been nothing resembling Anglo-Catholicism in ritual or dogma: worship took place in unadorned severity, and the great Bishop Butler, for keeping a crucifix, was suspected of being a secret Papist.

Johnson's politics also explain his severity towards Deists and free-thinkers. The Deist movement, which reached its height in the first three decades of the century and then died out, was in large part a political movement. Most of the Deists, from Toland to Tindal, were keen Whigs, and their campaign, which included criticism of the Biblical prophecies and miracles, was aimed at the political pretensions of the High Church party. Johnson always lumped free-thinkers and Whigs together as subversive of the *status quo*, and consequently of all morality. Another mark of Deism was the attempt to substitute 'Natural Law' and 'Natural Religion', common to all mankind, for the revelation of any particular religion. Johnson, who thought all talk of the 'natural' to be cant, particularly detested this aspect of Deism, which was represented most strongly by Rousseau. When Boswell, a secret Rousseauist or at least an admirer of 'natural' sexuality, tried to bring the conversation round to the Noble Savages of Otaheiti, Johnson would brush him off with 'Don't cant in defence of Savages.' Morality was for him only possible within the bounds of an established Church. Even if free-thinkers were not Whigs (and in fact after the mid-century the most eminent of them, Hume and Gibbon, were Tories), their morals were still not to be relied on. Boswell recorded this in the journal for 10th May 1776: 'Steevens said he would rather have character of Sodomite than Infidel. I, not; Johnson, yes. "An infidel would be so if he inclined."' Less brutally, he said of the sceptics: 'Truth is a cow which will yield such people no more milk, and so they are gone to milk the bull.'

Eighteenth-century England was far from being a Deistic nation. A higher proportion of the people than today went to Matins regularly on Sundays and to Communion at Easter. (Johnson, in going to Communion only once a year, did like almost everyone else.) The lower clergy mostly did their duty conscientiously on inadequate incomes; if some were farmers and others fox-hunters, their parishioners were not discontented. The cathedral chapters, like colleges and indeed all corporate bodies, were dormant, while the precious fabrics of stone and glass crumbled about their heads. Although Johnson reverenced the hierarchy, he was not particularly respectful to the actual bishops of his day; no doubt because most of them were political creatures, who neglected their dioceses to vote for the government in the House of Lords. 'No man', he said in 1775, 'can now be made a Bishop for his learning and piety; his only chance for promotion is his being connected with somebody who has parliamentary interest.'

The Nonconformist sects, who made up about a tenth of the population, had lost their old fire in preaching and politics, which had made the word 'enthusiasm' a term of abuse among the established majority. The Quakers had become what they are now, a small community of progressive industrialists; the other sects were moving towards placid Unitarianism. But because of their Whiggish, even regicidal, tradition, Johnson regarded the Scots Presbyterians with hostility and the English Dissenters with contempt. Towards the Methodists his attitude was ambiguous: he admired their diligence but thought that the Vice-Chancellor was right to expel Methodist undergraduates? ('A cow is a very good animal in the field; but we turn her out of a garden.') John Wesley was only the greatest of several evangelists who were converting the new industrial masses and the semi-pagan Welsh; while the peak of the Evangelical movement, which changed the character of English intellectual life, was not reached until after Johnson's death. Johnson knew John Wesley, and admired him as a conversationalist of his own calibre, but Wesley was 'always obliged to go at a certain hour. This is very disagreeable to a man who loves to fold his legs and have out his talk, as I do.'

To the much smaller minority of Roman Catholics Johnson was always well-disposed. Although critical over points of doctrine, and a jealous defender of the Church of England, he was not a militant Protestant, and would not have found much difficulty in worshipping according to the Roman rite. His disgust at the barbarous persecution of the Irish Catholics inspired his noblest political saying: 'Let the authority of the English government perish, rather than be maintained by iniquity.'

In his religion Johnson was to some extent a maker of England. He established himself as the popular image of a practical Christian, charitable and humane, and of a stern and kindly teacher. He could say truthfully of himself, 'Obscenity and Impiety have always been repressed in my company'; and, more effectively than any clergyman except Wesley, he set an example to hundreds who met him and thousands who read his works and life. Like his politics, Johnson's religion concealed a true liberalism beneath the dogmatic front; and in his broadmindedness, his learning and his common sense, he helped to further the best traditions of the Church of England.

In 1762 came his first recognition by the State, and indeed the only honour a government could then award to a private subject neither in Holy Orders nor active in trade or politics. There were no strings attached to the offer of a pension; and if he hesitated before accepting the offer, it was probably not because of the rude definition of 'pension' he had given in the *Dictionary*,[1] but because it meant a break with his anti-Hanoverian past—and no man enjoys cutting himself off from his rebellious youth. The Pension, of three hundred pounds a year, meant freedom from debt and enforced journalistic hack-work, freedom to set up his queer household of dependants, and above all freedom to travel. One of the first things he did to celebrate the Pension was to take a long trip to the west of England, in the company of Reynolds. Macaulay is responsible for the view that Johnson was a stay-at-home Londoner, and a despiser of foreign parts. But if he had not been away from London for more than a few days since 1755, that was because of poverty, not inclination. Henceforth, for the last twenty-two years of his life, he made a journey out of town almost every year. To Johnson the Wanderer the roads now lay open, to Wales, to Paris, and to Skye.

[1] 'In England it is generally understood to mean pay given to a state hireling for treason to his country.'

Chapter 5

MERIDIAN SPLENDOUR

5 MERIDIAN SPLENDOUR

1763–1772

> I drank tea at Davies's in Russell Street, and about seven came in the great Mr. Samuel Johnson, whom I have so long wished to see. Mr. Davies introduced me to him. As I knew his mortal antipathy at the Scotch, I cried to Davies, 'Don't tell where I come from.' However, he said, 'From Scotland.' 'Mr. Johnson,' said I, 'indeed I come from Scotland, but I cannot help it.' 'Sir,' replied he, 'that, I find, is what a very great many of your countrymen cannot help.' Mr. Johnson is a man of a most dreadful appearance. He is a very big man, is troubled with sore eyes, the palsy, and the king's evil. He is very slovenly in his dress and speaks with a most uncouth voice. Yet his knowledge and strength of expression command vast respect and render him very excellent company. He has great humour and is a worthy man. But his dogmatical roughness of manners is disagreeable. I shall mark what I remember of his conversation.—Boswell's *Journal*, 16th May 1763.

JAMES BOSWELL, aged twenty-two on this historic day, was already a practised writer of journals, with a memory for conversations like a tape-recorder. He was also one of the many Scots who swarmed into London in the early 'sixties, since George III had brought Lord Bute to power in 1762. The Scots were unpopular, as Boswell describes in his *London Journal*; and Johnson nourished an ancient prejudice against them. Boswell survived this powerful snub, and soon made friends with the great man. They met many times that summer, before Boswell left on the Grand Tour; Johnson did him the honour of travelling with him to Harwich, and their parting is described in one of the most moving pages of Boswell's *Life*.

> As the vessel put out to sea, I kept my eyes upon him for a considerable time, while he remained rolling his majestick frame in his usual manner, and at last I perceived him walk back to the town and he disappeared.

Johnson was not deceived by Boswell: he valued the young man's vitality and intelligence, and forgave him his brashness and folly. He must have known at an early stage that Boswell was recording his conversation, but made no objection; indeed he seems always to have regarded Boswell as a secretary for posterity, who saved him the labour of writing down thoughts which he knew to be valuable. Although he was sincerely fond of Boswell, their relationship was not the most intimate in either man's life. Johnson as a father-figure was a psychological necessity to Boswell, but Boswell did not play such an important part in Johnson's emotional life. Johnson, as we shall see, had much closer ties with the Thrales. There is no need to describe Boswell's complex character at greater length, since it is well enough known from the recently published *Private Papers*; to avoid misunderstanding, I should say that I consider him the greatest of biographers.

Boswell's absolute veracity in recording the *ipsissima verba* of conversations is well established. Occasionally he will tone down a sentence, where Johnson's language was too rough or frank, as can be seen by comparing the *Life* with the original journals. But we can be certain that Boswell not only gave Johnson's true views on every topic, but caught the essential flavour of his verbal wit, which deserves some analysis at this point. The most remarkable thing about this wit is its poetic quality: the best effects come from unforgettable visual images, usually in absurd juxtaposition. 'Sir, a woman's preaching is like a dog's walking on his hind legs. It is not done well, but you are surprised to find it done at all.'—that stays in the mind as a miniature poem, as does his scornful ending of a discussion on two minor poets, 'Sir, there is no settling the point of precedency between a louse and a flea.' By opposing concrete images to abstract theories, he deflates his opponents; this device may be called 'kicking the stone' from his famous refutation of Berkeley's idealism, and is used thus on another philosopher: 'But if he does really think that there is no distinction between virtue and vice, why, Sir, when he leaves our houses let us count our spoons.' Occasionally he reverses the process and moves from concrete to abstract, as in the description of Thrale's brewery: 'We are not here to sell a parcel of boilers and vats, but the potentiality of growing rich, beyond the dreams of avarice.' Some of his best strokes come from a magnificent use of climax, often at the end of the classical tripartite sentence. 'Claret is the liquor for boys; port for men; but he who aspires to the condition of a hero must drink brandy' is a fine example, but even more beautifully timed is his reply to Ogilvie, who observed that

> . . . Scotland had a great many noble prospects. JOHNSON: I believe, Sir, you have a great many. Norway, too, has noble wild prospects; and Lapland is remarkable for prodigious noble wild prospects. But, Sir, let me tell you, the noblest prospect which a Scotchman ever sees, is the high road that leads him to England!

Another rhetorical device is the neat antithesis of Augustan poetry, as when he said of a lady writer who had taken to using cosmetics, 'She is better employed at her toilet than using her pen. It is better she should be reddening her own cheeks, than blackening other people's characters.' The usual effect of his wit is reductive, and Johnson is a master at reducing everything to flat common sense, as in his reason for not climbing hills (he is 'content with knowing that by scrambling up a rock, I shall only see other rocks'), or his attack on the censorious which shows the great moralist's tolerance: 'You don't call a man an ironmonger for buying and selling a pen-knife; so you don't call a man a whoremonger for getting one wench with child.'

Finally, he showed himself a master of invective, when he routed an insolent Thames water-man with an elaborate insult: 'Sir, your wife, under pretence of keeping a bawdy house, is a receiver of stolen goods.' Thus from Boswell, and almost only from Boswell, we can see the restless working of Johnson's imagination, which created an incomparable vehicle for the teaching of wisdom.

The next important event in Johnson's life took place in the winter of 1763–64. Apparently at his suggestion a number of his friends formed the Club, a small literary society which was to become an assembly of the most distinguished men of the age. The eighteenth century was the age of clubs: whereas nearly all official or responsible societies went into a decline, great vigour was shown in founding private associations of gentlemen, who met at White's for gambling, at Freemasons' lodges for drinking, and in many small groups for good fellowship and solid conversation. The original nine brethren of the Club included Joshua Reynolds, the prime mover, and Johnson's other old friends, Beauclerk, Langton, and Hawkins. (The last, 'a most unclubbable man', left after a few years.) To these were added two newer friends of brilliance, Oliver Goldsmith, with whose literary work Johnson was now closely associated, and Edmund Burke, the only man in England to rival Johnson in discussion. Rather later they elected Garrick, then at the height of his fame, Thomas Warton, and Adam Smith; and by the end of Johnson's life the members included Bishop Percy, Charles James Fox, R. B. Sheridan, Gibbon, Sir William Jones the orientalist, Dr Burney the musician, and Malone the critic, besides a sprinkling of noblemen and bishops, and of course James Boswell. The striking thing about most of the members is that they were 'new men'. 'Men are every day starting up from obscurity to wealth', said Johnson, and this could be applied not only to the new industrial entrepreneurs but to some of his fellow-members; men of relatively humble origin, who had made their way in an oligarchic and stratified society by means of their learning and literature. Burke, Goldsmith, and Sheridan came from the subject and hungry land of Ireland; Adam Smith and Boswell represented the ambitious Scots; and Reynolds and Percy, like Johnson himself, were provincials of the lower middle-class. In the company of these men, Johnson's powers of debate were called forth to their full extent, and there he enjoyed the only form of democracy that meant anything to him—a sodality of equals.

In 1764, spurred on by the satire of Charles Churchill ('He for subscribers baits his hook, And takes your cash; but where's the book?'), he returned to hard work on his edition of Shakespeare, and managed to get it to the publishers at last in the following year. As a work of scholarship it was not a success: his attempt to establish the text from the Quartos and Folios was perfunctory, and unworthy of the century of Bentley and Porson. But as literary criticism the 'Preface' and some of the notes are supreme, and must be considered along with his other masterpiece the *Lives of the Poets*, in a later chapter. In 1765 he also received the degree of Ll.D. from Trinity College, Dublin, and was henceforth Doctor Johnson. In

13 The house of Thomas Davies, the print-seller of Covent Garden, where Johnson and Boswell first met

From a print by C. J. Smith

14 Mrs. Thrale

From a portrait, made by George Dance in 1793, after her marriage to Gabriel Piozzi

January of that year there occurred the event which was to change the whole course of his life: Arthur Murphy introduced him to the Thrales, who became his greatest friends and more than friends. Boswell through jealousy—and this is the only reproach that can be cast against his biography—deliberately obscured the part played by the Thrales; for it was to them that Johnson gave his heart.

Henry Thrale was the son of a self-made brewer. He was handsome, well educated, at Oxford and on the Grand Tour, possessed of extremely good manners, a rake and a glutton, a connoisseur of literature and the arts, and successful in business. In 1763 he married Hester Lynch Salusbury, of a good Welsh family. Her character cannot be described in a sentence; but its outstanding traits were kindliness and energy. During the first fifteen years of her marriage she bore Thrale twelve children, only four of whom survived childhood. Despite the fact that she was pregnant almost all the time, she fulfilled an ambitious social and literary programme. She had little in common with her husband besides a taste for literature and literary men, and he was notoriously unfaithful to her; but their marriage was a happy one. They lived both at Southwark by the brewery, and at Streatham Park, a small country house which grew in size and splendour as the profits of beer mounted. Unusually, the first meeting with Johnson was a success, and he soon became a regular diner, and then an adopted member of the household. The bond became closer when Johnson suffered a severe mental illness, almost a complete breakdown, in 1766. To the Thrales he admitted his fear of insanity and in his agony of depression confessed his secret guilt or fantasies of guilt. Mrs Thrale remembered how 'my husband involuntarily lifted up one hand to shut his mouth, from provocation at having a man so wildly proclaim what he could at last persuade no one to believe; and what, if true, would have been so very unfit to reveal.' The Thrales took him to Streatham for part of that year, and nursed him devotedly back to health; and during the next sixteen years he lived with them for most of the time, at Streatham, Southwark, or Brighton or on long excursions. He always called his host and hostess 'Master' and 'Mistress' and indeed Thrale was the only one who could keep him in order. He saw to it that Johnson, no lover of clean linen, was tolerably well washed and dressed: he even had a servant stand waiting with a fresh wig, to replace the one Johnson would burn as he bent over a candle to read. He could control the flow of conversation, saying what a host should say to his learned guests at all times: 'There, there, now we have enough for one lecture, Dr. Johnson; we will not be upon education any more till after dinner, if you please.'

If Thrale was not a brilliant talker, he was the perfect host to those who were. 'Why, Sir,' said Johnson, 'his conversation does not show the minute hand; but he strikes the hour very correctly.' Drawn by Johnson's presence, the charm of the Thrales, and the luxury of the household, some of the best and cleverest company in England came to Streatham. Soon it was almost a second home for the Club, with Reynolds, Burke, Goldsmith, and Garrick as frequent guests. With them came Giuseppe Marc' Antonio Baretti, a scholar and journalist whose personality was evidently more impressive than his writings: when he was tried for manslaughter in 1769, Johnson and his distinguished friends testified to his good character. It is not surprising that Mrs Thrale soon took to recording what she heard at her table. Her early journals are almost wholly lost, but she copied extracts from them into her *Thraliana*, which she began in 1776; as raw material her notes are second only to Boswell's *Private Papers*. Thanks to her inexhaustible vitality, she could listen to Johnson until the small hours, pouring his tea from a three-quart pot. Johnson slept badly and did not like to be left alone at night; the diuretic and stimulant effect of the tea, not to speak of indigestion from his voracious over-eating, only made his condition worse. But in other ways his health improved: he was given a balanced diet, with the fresh fruit and vegetables that he loved, and made to take exercise. At Brighton he rode and bathed, earning the praise of William Gerard Hamilton, 'Why Johnson rides as well, for aught I see, as the most illiterate fellow in England.' His chronic bronchitis was thus kept at bay, but he still suffered regularly from fits of depression, becoming more and more dependent on Mrs Thrale as his nurse or lay-analyst. About 1768 he entrusted her 'with a Secret far dearer to him than his life'. What this secret was has not been discovered, but speculation has been aroused by a reference in his journal to insane thoughts about fetters, by an item in Mrs Thrale's effects listed as 'Johnson's padlock' and by a strange and cryptic letter in French to Mrs Thrale, dated as about 1773.

Johnson concerned himself with all the affairs of the Thrale household. He worked on a translation of Boethius with Mrs Thrale, and annotated her verses. Together they took up Johnson's old pursuit of chemistry, and planned to make a kind of laboratory at Streatham. They got as far as some disastrous experiments with smelting minerals in 1771, when Henry Thrale put a stop to this dangerous occupation. Johnson bought books for the Thrales' library, supervised the education of the children, and even became concerned with the brewery. In 1772 as the result of some unwise gambling on a new process Thrale lost a great deal of money. Johnson spent much time worrying about Thrale's business problems, and discussing the price of barley and malt; while Mrs Thrale saved the situation by borrowing heavily from her family. The crisis was soon past and the brewery began to prosper again, but from this time onwards both Johnson and Mrs Thrale were involved in its management. Johnson had no difficulty in grasping the technical side of any industry, and his experience of money-making prompted his classic remark, 'Trade could not be managed by those who manage it if it had much difficulty.'

Johnson's closest identification with Henry Thrale was in politics. But for this friendship it is unlikely that Johnson would have ever again taken much interest in public affairs, which as he told Boswell 'vex no man'. His old Jacobite and High Tory views had, as we have seen, cooled almost to zero in the 'fifties. He knew as well as anyone that the issues of his youth, Hanoverians versus legitimists, Dr Sacheverell and Bishop Hoadley, Big-Endians and Little-Endians, were now dead, and he had no wish to follow an antique drum. Politics no longer, he thought, involved matters of principle, but 'are now nothing more than means of rising in the world'. Only loyalty to Thrale brought him back to the battle, and this is in the wholly practical capacity of election agent; only later was his theoretical interest aroused. Not long after their meeting in 1765, Thrale stood as a candidate for Southwark in a by-election. Johnson helped him by drafting an appeal to the electors and other propaganda. On that occasion Thrale was returned without opposition, but three years later his election was contested with some violence. By now the Wilkesites were active in Southwark, while Thrale was a loyal supporter of the Government and the Court party. Johnson again helped in writing addresses and running the campaign, and Thrale was re-elected. Two years later Johnson wrote the first of his four famous political pamphlets, *The False Alarm*. It is unlikely that the pension had anything to do with this, since it had been explained on its granting that Johnson would incur no obligation to write for the Governmental side. Clifford thinks it likely that *The False Alarm* was written only after Thrale's urging. By this time Johnson had gained some reputation as a practical politician, and there was even a scheme, which came to nothing, for getting him into Parliament. Shortly after he had published, with the Ministry's encouragement, *Thoughts on the late Transactions respecting Falkland's Islands* (1771) he was recommended by William Strahan, printer and M.P., who, knowing Johnson's reputation, explained, 'Nor is any thing to be apprehended from the supposed impetuosity of his temper. To the friends of the King you will find him a lamb, to his enemies a lion.' The Ministry, however, was too nervous to accept the suggestion. To give an outline of Johnson's political career as a whole, I must go outside the time limits of this chapter. In 1774 there was another election in which Thrale had a serious struggle against the Wilkesites; there was rioting at Southwark, the 'mob' taking the side of the 'Patriots'. Johnson drafted at least one of Thrale's addresses, and then wrote *The Patriot* at great speed: 'it was called for by my political friends on Friday, was written on Saturday'. He went with Mrs Thrale on her canvassing expeditions, and enjoyed the rough jostle of the hustings.

> At the same Election an ordinary Fellow—a Hatter who was zealous for our Cause came suddenly up to Johnson and embracing him cried out—Ah Sir 'tis no Time now to mind making of *Hats*! I was frighted, & thought the Doctor would be embarrassed by this half-drunken Hero;—But he with the utmost presence of Mind made answer in the same gay Tone, No Sir—Hats are of no use to us now but to throw up in the Air & huzza with.—[throwing up his own, Mrs Thrale later added.]

In 1775 the American War was beginning, and Johnson defended the Government's policy with peculiar enthusiasm in the last of his pamphlets, *Taxation No Tyranny*. The disasters of the war and the incompetence of Lord North's administration must have cooled his zeal; but if he wrote no more pamphlets he still remained loyal to

Thrale. Thrale's chances of being re-elected in 1780 were ruined by his hopeless state of health. Johnson joined Mrs Thrale in canvassing votes and did other election work, even though he was busy with the *Lives of the Poets*; but this time to no avail. After Thrale's defeat and death Johnson's political comments are few and subdued.

The political situation from 1762 to 1780 has been described as the crisis of the *ancien régime* in England; the constitutional troubles at home and the Rebellion in America were part of an Atlantic Revolution, which reached France in 1789. The fundamental issue was the share-out of political power. The economic development of England had produced new groups that had ambitions and vigour but very little share in the government of their country, groups such as merchants, industrialists, professional men, and above all American colonists. The mechanism of government was an inheritance from the old patriarchal way of life. The King was expected to govern personally through his Ministers, his personal servants whom he chose himself. In choosing them he was expected to give a share of power to the great landed magnates, who formed alliances or 'connexions', and controlled blocks of voters in both Houses. England was not a democracy, and there were no political parties in the modern sense, merely groups of politicians united by family and territorial links, and more remotely by vague 'Whig' or 'Tory' principles. The most important of these groups was the Court party, whose emoluments depended on the Crown and whose policy was consequently to be relied on. No government in the eighteenth century ever lost a general election: changes of ministry took place in between elections, when the King or the leading connexions withdrew their support. The House of Commons, elected by a small and unfairly distributed suffrage, was usually easy to control, although it did contain a number of sometimes restive country gentlemen and a few genuine independents like Edmund Burke. All oppositions, like Johnson in his youth, inveighed against 'corruption', i.e. the distribution of money and favours to keep potential opposition in check, and all governments used it. This system had worked well enough for seventy years, as long as there was a King like William III or a Minister like Walpole able enough to control and placate the various groupings, and as long as the class structure was stable enough for the rulers to understand it. It broke down under George III because it could no longer satisfy the aspirations of new social groupings; and it broke down all the faster because the King stubbornly insisted on choosing incompetent ministers. One blunder succeeded another. In 1763 the Grenville ministry mishandled the first proceedings against Wilkes, and began to irritate the Americans by stupid legislation. The Duke of Grafton's Ministry of 1766 aggravated the errors of its predecessors by insisting on the right to tax the American colonies, and on Wilkes's return in 1768 panicked. As a result of the outcry about the Middlesex election and Wilkes's expulsion, Grafton fell in 1770. He was succeeded by Lord North, the most unsuccessful statesman of the century, whose incompetence led to the disgraces of the American War, and to the almost complete breakdown of 1780. At each stage in this dismal chronicle, the feeling of imminent doom only drew together the more closely all who stood for the old way of life: the King, his Ministers, a majority of both Houses, and probably most of the population—and Samuel Johnson. If Toryism in Johnson's youth meant a dream of the Middle Ages, of a godlike prince surrounded by vassals and bishops, Toryism now meant no more than the defence of the established citadel against the unknown and largely unseen enemy, social change.

If the Government's supporters hardly knew what they were standing for, no more did the opposition. Wilkes had no clear policy, and began simply by attacking Bute's peace policy in the interests of the Pitt connexion and of the City merchants, who were imperially minded. He unwittingly became a hero and a symbol when the Government acted against him. Their first proceedings against him were of doubtful, their later actions over the Middlesex election of certain illegality. They had blundered into exploding the charge of great force in English politics, the defence of the English Law and the liberty of the subject. 'Wilkes and Liberty' became a slogan around which every kind of discontent with the old order crystallized, not only at home but in America. This was the beginning of the reforming movement among the Whig connexions, and the extra-parliamentary radical societies, which began to gain strength from the 'seventies. Since Johnson confines himself to defending Governmental actions which were transparently illegal and inexpedient, his pamphlets *The False Alarm* and *The Patriot* are merely ingenious pleading in good prose. He was unable to raise any general issues or to take the topic on to the higher plane of political theory, as his friend and opponent Burke could do in *Thoughts upon the Present Discontents* (1770). For once, Johnson had taken up a subject that he could not or would not understand.

His third pamphlet, on *Falkland's Islands*, is about quite a minor point, but became a defence of the Government's peace policy. Johnson revived the old Tory dislike of militarism, which is most powerfully expressed in *Gulliver's Travels*, and he speaks on a subject in which his heart and his head were deeply engaged. Because of our experience of total war we may be inclined to look back nostalgically on the relatively polite and restrained wars of the eighteenth century, fought with good manners and limited objectives. Gibbon sometimes makes a complacent comparison between gentlemanly Augustan battles and the fanatic massacres of the past. But Johnson reminds us of the truth about war in his time, in a passage which shows his immense sympathy and grasp of reality:

> The life of a modern soldier is ill represented by heroick fiction. War has means of destruction more formidable than the cannon and the sword. Of the thousands and ten thousands, that perished in our late contests with France and Spain, a very small part ever felt the stroke of an enemy; the rest languished in tents and ships, amidst damps and putrefaction; pale, torpid, spiritless, and helpless; gasping and groaning, unpitied among men, made obdurate by long continuance of hopeless misery, and whelmed in pits, or heaved into the ocean, without notice and without remembrance. By incommodious encampments and unwholesome stations, where courage is useless, and enterprise unpracticable, fleets are silently dispeopled, and armies sluggishly melted away.

In his comments on America, however, Johnson does raise issues of great interest. These are to be found in his conversation and in other writings besides *Taxation no Tyranny: an Answer to the Resolutions and Address of the American Congress*. The American Revolution had a great many aspects, only some of which concerned Johnson. There were the legal and constitutional arguments concerning taxation and representation, about which he was privately not very sure, as his letters show, although he publicly trumpeted in defence of them. The American Revolution was also a true liberal revolution, an attempt to change the old social structure, which has made the United States, in one sense, a classless society. To this Johnson, in so far as he understood it, was opposed, as much as to Rousseau or any kind of radicalism based on an optimistic view of human nature. To that extent he was an enemy of liberty. But the Revolution was also a revolt of 'colons', analagous to that which brought De Gaulle to power in 1958: the settlers wanted to enjoy the profits of African slave labour without any possible interference from a metropolitan government. Not that England was above reproach where the slave trade was concerned; but Johnson's attitude was an encouragement to the abolitionists, who had their way in a few decades. He had a life-long detestation of slavery, affirming in 1740 'the natural right of the negroes to liberty and independence'. He sincerely believed that the Americans, because they were slave-owners, deserved no sympathy at all: 'How is it that we hear the loudest *yelps* for liberty among the drivers of negroes?' he asked, and called 'the planters of America, a race of mortals whom, I suppose, no other man wishes to resemble.' He gave a toast 'in company with some very grave men at Oxford. . . . "Here's to the next insurrection of the negroes in the West Indies!"'

Johnson's attitude to the English ascendancy in Ireland was precisely the same. In 1773, 'bursting forth with a generous indignation', he said, 'the Irish are in a most unnatural state; for we see there the minority prevailing over the majority'; and to the Irish Dr Maxwell he 'severely reprobated the barbarous debilitating policy of the British government, which, he said, was a most detestable mode of persecution. . . . Let the authority of the English government perish, rather than be maintained by iniquity.' In his defence of the oppressed, Johnson was a true liberal. His has nothing to do with the bogus liberalism that sympathizes with nations well able to look after themselves, whether Boer, Nazi German, or Communist Russian. This has a parallel in his approach to individuals. Mrs Thrale often records his strange indifference, even callousness, about the troubles of the rich and educated (which, after all, may be very real troubles), and she contrasts it with his unlimited sympathy for the poor.

> He loved the poor as I never saw any one else do, with an earnest desire to make them happy—What signifies, says some one, giving halfpence

> to common beggars? They only lay it out in gin and tobacco. 'And why should they be denied such sweetness of their existence (says Johnson)? it is surely very savage to refuse them every possible avenue to pleasure, reckoned too coarse for our own acceptance.'

He was never optimistic about what could be done to relieve oppression or poverty by political means. We are born into 'a world bursting with sin and sorrow' and it is always our duty to make it better. This can be done only by a series of limited campaigns, such as the one fought for the abolition of slavery and the reform of the criminal law. Johnson's contributions to these make up his legacy to the English liberal tradition.

If Johnson often impatiently dismissed the views of Whigs, Wilkesites, and other factious dogs, it was because he believed that they had really nothing to complain of. Whatever they might say, liberty in the England of his day was *not* in danger, and talk about tyranny was cant. But if there had been real oppression, he would have invoked the principle of the great Whig Locke, that 'there remains still in the people a supreme power to remove or alter the legislature'. However great his veneration of the established order, Johnson always allowed an appeal to moral truth as more valid than any political loyalty. He said to Sir Adam Fergusson, 'I consider that in no government power can be abused long. Mankind will not bear it. If a sovereign oppresses his people to a great degree they will rise and cut off his head. There is a remedy in human nature against tyranny, that will keep us safe under every form of government'; and even more forcibly to Boswell: 'If the abuse be enormous, Nature will rise up, and claiming her original rights, overturn a corrupt political system.'

Johnson's political activities did not take up all his time until 1773, nor was he always in company with the Thrales. Boswell, on his return from the Continent in 1766, saw him in town, and visited him again in '68, '69, '72, and early in '73; although the record of those years makes up only a small part of the *Life*. The most striking incident was his interview with George III in '67, in which the King acquitted himself surprisingly well: 'Johnson showed himself highly pleased with his Majesty's conversation and gracious behaviour.' After his Shakespeare, he wrote little beside the political tracts, but in '71 and '72 worked on the revision of the *Dictionary*. He travelled a good deal, both with and without the Thrales, spending some time at Lichfield, Ashbourne, and Oxford. In these years he tasted the sweetness of life, and walked in glory, marching 'to kettle-drum and trumpets' in conversation and rolling his majestic frame down the pavements of Fleet Street.

15 Boswell
After a sketch by George Langton

Chapter 6

THE HEBRIDES; DR DODD

6 THE HEBRIDES; Dr Dodd

1773–1777

IN 1773 there took place the event for which Boswell had been hoping and planning ever since he first met Johnson: the tour to the Hebrides. Boswell's wish to make this tour himself sprang from his sentimental Jacobite feelings about the '45 Rebellion, and from the romantic attraction that the Highlands exercise on any Lowland Scot; and he wanted to make the startling experiment of placing the sage of Fleet Street in the least urban surroundings imaginable. Johnson had been interested but as usual procrastinated, and even after plans had been made in the spring of 1773 showed no hurry to join Boswell in Edinburgh. His coach did not reach the city until the 14th of August, which was too late in the season for such a trip: as we shall see, they were lucky not to have been drowned in the equinoctial gales. Boswell records in his journal the excitement he felt at having the great man walk arm-in-arm with him up the High Street, a filthy canyon between black tenements: 'I smell you in the dark,' was Johnson's apostrophe. Two days later Boswell wrote to Lord Elibank:[1]

> Mr. Samuel Johnson is at length under my roof. I know you would never forgive me if I delayed a single post to inform you of the joyful & valuable news. Pray come to us tomorrow. We are going to the Highlands & the Hebrides, and shall then return to Edinburgh; and you may be sure will pass a night or two at your Lordships. In the mean

[1] Unpublished letter, printed here by permission of the owner.

> time *ipse veni.* Give us no such letters as that which you wrote to one of your sisters who wanted to come and live with you, & which you read to me. Robertson dined with Johnson today. Fergusson sups with him. So he has better than mere *oaten* Professeurs.

Elibank, one of the leading figures among the Edinburgh *literati*, had replied to Johnson's definition of oats as a food for men in Scotland, for horses in England, 'Very true, and where will you find such *men* and such *horses*?' He could not meet them until their return, but meanwhile Boswell lost no time in showing off the great man to the other men of letters in his distinguished circle. To the intellectual glories of Edinburgh Johnson remained somewhat indifferent.

It took them eleven days of travel to reach the Highlands. On the way they visited the universities of St. Andrews and Aberdeen, but little stirred Johnson's imagination except the ruins of Arbroath Abbey. When they crossed the 'Highland line' near Inverness, they entered a different world, to which no poet can fail to respond. The Highlands had been stripped of their forest cover, to provide charcoal for iron-making, and must have looked as bare as they did thirty years ago, before the Forestry Commission began to reclothe some of the slopes. With the forests much of the wild life had disappeared, and the last wolf had been killed earlier in the century. The black-faced sheep had not been introduced; such wealth as there was lay in cattle rather than in the wretched crops. The people were poor in almost everything except pride, charming manners, and folk-lore. You can still see cottages of the kind described by Johnson, their thatch held down by boulders. There were no towns, except on Lewis, and no proper tracks even for riding, except a few made by General Wade in recent years. The traditional dress (the plaid, a blanket worn over the kilt) and the carrying of arms had been forbidden since the '45; these were part of the decay of the ancient way of life. The clan system was breaking down, as the fighting chiefs turned themselves into fashionable gentlemen and rapacious landlords. Emigration to America had begun, though not on the scale it reached in the nineteenth century with the evictions and potato famine. The climate was wet and windy but mild enough (semi-tropical plants like palms can be grown in some of the places Johnson passed); but there had been a Black Spring in

1771 which had increased the distress of a peasantry too backward to make good use of their limited resources.

Into this new world the travellers rode, on a fine August day. They travelled down the military road on the south side of Loch Ness, with two Highlanders running before them. Soon they had their first sight of a crofter's hut, where the woman of the house thought that Johnson had designs on her virtue: Moray Maclaren thinks that she remembered only too well the English troops after Culloden. Later they came to the celebrated waterfall of Foyers, where the country 'strikes the imagination with all the gloom and grandeur of Siberian solitude'. But the river was too low to be spectacular,

> and we were left to exercise our thoughts, by endeavouring to conceive the effect of a thousand streams poured from the mountains into one channel, struggling for expansion in a narrow passage, exasperated by rocks rising in their way, and at last discharging all the violence of waters by a sudden fall through the horrid chasm.

—Johnson's imagination as usual preferred the ideal to the disappointments of the real. After staying a night with the garrison at Fort Augustus, they took the military road over the hills to Glen Moriston, and thence to Glenshiel; on the way Johnson dismissed a mountain as 'a considerable protuberance', and had a delicious rest:

> I sat down on a bank, such a writer of Romance might have delighted to feign. I had indeed no trees to whisper over my head, but a clear rivulet streamed at my feet. The day was calm, the air soft, and all was rudeness, silence, and solitude. Before me, and on either side, were high hills, which by hindering the eye from ranging, forced the mind to find entertainment for itself. Whether I spent the hour well I know not; for here I first conceived the thought of this narration.

The ascent of the Mam Rattachan was the only part of the journey by land when Johnson thought himself in any danger: to cheer him up, one of the men 'cried, with a very Highland accent, "See, such pretty goats!" Then he whistled *whu*! and made them jump.' Johnson was out of humour and had his only quarrel with Boswell on the trip, caused by the latter riding on ahead to Glenelg. At all other times he was the ideal traveller, impervious to discomfort, even accepting philosophically the discovery in their bedroom at

Glenelg 'a man black as a Cyclops from the forge'. On the next day they took a boat to Skye, where, except for Macdonald's meanness, all was warm hospitality and good cheer.

It is unnecessary to follow the rest of their journey in detail, through the various houses of Skye, to Dunvegan, the farthest north that they reached. Here Boswell and Johnson both wrote to Lord Elibank: Johnson's letter is given in the *Journal* but Boswell's has only recently come to light:[1]

> No earlier than the day before yesterday I had the honour to receive your Lordship's most agreeable letter, which was a rich cordial I do assure you. Mr. Johnson has stood every fatigue & every inconvenience with heroick philosophy. We are now at the Laird of Macleod's old castle in the Isle of Sky, from whence we purpose going to the Islands of Mull and Icolmkill. We then shall land in Lorn & proceed to Inverary, Glasgow and Auchinleck which we hope to reach by the 8th. or 10th. of October. We shall repose as long there as I can prevail with Mr. Johnson to stay, & then return to Edinburgh where I take it we may be about the 20th. of October. If your Lordship finds it convenient to meet us at Glasgow the third or fourth of October at the Saracen's Head we shall be happy, and you may judge if your old acquaintance my father will not make you welcome. If you cannot do that, you may depend on my informing you of the day on which we will be at Edinburgh and I look forward with joy to the hours that we shall pass there & at Barncrieff.

Boswell's time-table, as Johnson expected, went wrong. Attempting to cross from Skye to Mull they were nearly drowned, because of a storm and a thoroughly Highland muddle, and had to put in at Coll for ten days. Mull was less interesting than Skye, except for the visit on the 20th of October to the monastic ruins of Iona. To Iona Johnson's response was fervently expressed:

> We were now treading that illustrious Island, which was once the luminary of the *Caledonian* regions, whence savage clans and roving barbarians derived the benefits of knowledge, and the blessings of religion. To abstract the mind from all local emotion would be impossible, if it were endeavoured, and would be foolish, if it were possible. Whatever withdraws us from the power of our senses; whatever makes the past, the distant, or the future predominate over the present, advances us in the dignity of thinking beings. Far from me and from my friends, be such frigid philosophy as may conduct us indifferent and unmoved over any ground that has been dignified by wisdom,

[1] Hitherto unpublished: printed here by permission of the owner.

Jan. 1. 1766. after two in the morning.

Almighty and most merciful Father,
I again appear in thy presence the wretched
mispender of another year which thy mercy has allowed me. O Lord let me not sink
into total depravity, look down upon me, and
rescue me at last from the captivity of Sin.
Impart to me good resolutions, and give me
strength and perseverance to perform them.
Take not from me thy Holy Spirit but grant
that I may redeem the time lost, and that by temperance and diligence, by Sincere Repentance and faithful Obedience
I may finally obtain everlasting happiness
for the Sake of Jesus Christ, our Lord. Amen

16 A prayer, written on "Jan. 1, 1766, after two in the morning"
From Prayers and Meditations

17 The Recovery: "I awakened at noon with a severe headache. . . ."

18 Setting out from Edinburgh

From caricatures by Thomas Rowlandson

> bravery, or virtue. That man is little to be envied, whose patriotism would not gain force upon the plain of *Marathon*, or whose piety would not grow warmer among the ruins of *Iona*.

Their return south via Inveraray (where they were well entertained by the Duke, and Boswell snubbed by the Duchess of Argyll), Loch Lomond, and Glasgow was not so rewarding. At Auchinleck Johnson became involved in violent controversy with Boswell's father, a Presbyterian Whig, over religion and politics. Boswell was evidently too shocked by this conflict to record the details in his journal, so we have to fall back on Walter Scott's perhaps apocryphal story. When Johnson in fury asked what good Cromwell had ever done to his country, Lord Auchinleck replied: 'God, Doctor! he gart kings ken that they had a lith in their neck' (*anglice*, he taught kings they had a joint in their neck).

Boswell's *The Journal of a Tour to the Hebrides*, published in 1785, after Johnson's death, is one of the finest travel books ever written. Boswell's spontaneous gaiety is the setting for his romantic quest of memories of Prince Charles, and his heroic-comic picture of Johnson in a series of new human situations. *The Journal of a Tour to the Hebrides* is more visually brilliant than the *Life*, and less sordid and egoistic than the other journals. It is even better in the manuscript version, discovered in a croquet box at Malahide Castle in 1930, and edited by Pottle and Bennett. Before Malone made Boswell prune it, the journal contained, besides a mass of fascinating information about people, food and drink, many interesting things about Johnson: his strong language on occasions, his remarks on privies ('He said if ever a man thinks at all, it is there. He generally thinks then with great intenseness'), his malicious mimicry of the absurd Lady Macdonald. Here Boswell comes nearest to presenting the complete man.

Johnson's *A Journey to the Western Islands of Scotland*, published two years after the event, is not a brilliant travel book. It shows a notable lack of warm and intimate response to landscape and to people. Johnson's prose is not a satisfactory medium for recording visual impressions of new scenes. It is not that he did not enjoy the mountains—his Latin poem on Skye, sent to Mrs Thrale, shows that he did—or that he did not like the people he met. But it was not to his purpose to offer a traveller's personal commentary; instead, he tried to write a kind of social and economic survey, and to understand Highland life. In this he was largely successful, although he had difficulty in getting at the truth. The Highlanders, preferring politeness to accuracy, rarely gave him a straight answer, and no two accounts or explanations ever tallied. Johnson approached everything with his profound scepticism, which was justified about the authenticity of Macpherson's *Ossian*, if not about the depth of Loch Ness. Weighing up the evidence judiciously, he goes into questions of economics, agriculture and trade, showing a fine grasp of every process he describes, such as the building of cottages and the use of seaweed as compost. He discusses the need for and the difficulties of reafforestation with particular thoroughness and drawing apparently sound conclusions. From economics he goes on to the social structure of the Gaels: there are many anecdotes about clan history, but these are meant not to be picturesque but to show how the clan system worked and how it is changing. This leads him on to recent history, and the consequences of the '45: the decline of the military role of the Highlanders and their blood-feuds, after the ban on carrying arms was enforced; the transformation of the hereditary chiefs into modern landlords; the pros and cons of emigration; the means of maintaining law and order. The result is a complete and sane view of the Highland problem, perhaps unequalled until the recent *West Highland Survey*, edited by Frazer Darling. Throughout his examination Johnson shows himself as resolutely anti-primitivist, refusing to treat the Highlanders as happy or virtuous children of nature, or noble savages, though giving them their due for courage and civility. He will not even over-praise the natural beauty of peasant women, saying in a profound aside: 'To expand the human face to its full perfection, it seems necessary that the mind should co-operate by placidness of content, or consciousness of superiority.' But as always he is sympathetic to poverty and to the boredom produced by poverty. If his journey has taken on the subdued tone of Rasselas's wanderings, it also ends on a note of cautious encouragement, where he describes an Edinburgh school for the deaf and dumb:

> It was pleasing to see one of the most desperate of human calamities capable of so much help: whatever enlarges hope, will exalt courage; after having seen the deaf taught arithmetic, who would be afraid to cultivate the Hebrides?

There were other wanderings during the next four years, besides the regular visits to Lichfield and Ashbourne. The Thrales, more prosperous than ever, took Johnson to North Wales in the summer of 1774. This trip was not a complete success, since Johnson was sometimes 'churlish and irritable'. The diary he kept is short and perfunctory, and although he saw Chatsworth, Kedleston, and Blenheim, like any twentieth-century tourist, he seemed bored with these great houses and their gardens. His Philistinism unfortunately forbids a biographer to write about the greatest achievement of eighteenth-century culture, these palaces of stone and glass, harmonized with the surrounding country by the skill of the landscape gardeners: it was the moment in time when the Earthly Paradise, for the happy few, came nearest to being realized. To wild scenery Johnson responded more keenly. A passage about Hawkstone Park in Derbyshire, which looks like a draft of an essay, shows Johnson in as 'romantic' a mood as any of the late-eighteenth-century travellers, enjoying the pleasing horror of the wilderness; but for the formality of the phrasing this might almost be Gray in the Lake District:

> Though it wants water it excells Dovedale, by the extent of its prospects, the awfulness of its shades, the horrors of its precipices, the verdure of its hollows and the loftiness of its rocks. The Ideas which it forces upon the mind, are the sublime, the dreadful, and the vast. Above, is inaccessible altitude, below, is horrible profundity. . . . He that mounts the precipices at Hawkestone, wonders how he came hither, and doubts how he shall return. His walk is an adventure, and his departure an escape. He has not the tranquillity, but the horrour of solitude, a kind of turbulent pleasure between fright and admiration.

In the autumn of the next year he paid his only visit to the Continent, spending a month in Paris with the Thrales and Baretti. Although he could write good French, he conversed with the learned men he met only in Latin. Again he kept a short diary, which adds little to our knowledge of Johnson or of France. He notes his admiration of the Raphaels in the Palais Royal, but was obviously more interested in the libraries and technical matters like the making of looking-glasses. With French culture he was not impressed, and his comments to Boswell on his return echo the usual complaints of English travellers: he found the French 'an indelicate people; they will spit on any place'; a footman blew down the spout of the teapot and sugared his coffee with his fingers; 'I was going to put it aside; but hearing it was made on purpose for me, I e'en tasted Tom's fingers'. But Johnson could put up with such discomforts, and had caught the strong contagion of wandering. He was delighted when the Thrales planned an even more ambitious trip to Italy for 1776; and was sadly disappointed when this had to be abandoned, because of the death of Thrale's only son. He had to be content with a few weeks in Bath and an excursion to Bristol with Boswell. Thenceforward his health and work and the Thrales' fortunes prevented him from travelling abroad, but during every remaining year of his life he made at least one journey out of London. 'If I had no duties, and no reference to futurity, I would spend my life driving briskly in a post-chaise with a pretty woman', he told Boswell. Despite his lack of opportunity, Johnson took his place among that stoical and inquisitive band of English travellers who astonished the world.

Apart from politics and travel, these years passed uneventfully. Johnson published little besides *A Journey to the Western Islands* and political propaganda. In 1775 he received an honorary Ll.D. from Oxford, though even then he would not call himself 'Doctor'. He met Mrs Montagu and the Blue-Stockings, and later the most remarkable of the literary ladies, Fanny Burney. He saw Boswell every year from '75 to '79, and these are the most brilliant pages of the *Life*. In March 1777 he contracted with a syndicate of booksellers to write what he described as 'little Lives, and little Prefaces, to a little edition of the English Poets'. But before he started on the crowning work of his life, he became involved in the fate of Dr Dodd the forger—an episode which reveals one of Johnson's least-known services to civilization, in the unexpected field of legal reform.

Johnson had long been interested in the law. Professor E. L. McAdam, to whom we owe most of our knowledge of this aspect of Johnson, calls him 'the greatest lawyer-layman of the century'. To most laymen the legal mind is an even greater mystery than the scientific mind, but it appears that Johnson possessed both. He told Boswell, 'I ought to have been a lawyer'; and when another friend said that he might have become Lord Chancellor, he replied with feeling, 'Why will you vex me by suggesting this, when it is too late?' His poverty and lack of a degree had prevented him from going into the legal or any other profession; but he began to study law in his Grub-Street days. He wrote an opinion for Cave on a question of copyright, then improved his knowledge of constitutional matters when writing the Parliamentary Debates. The *Dictionary* shows that he had read almost as many legal as scientific books, in search of accurate definitions. The only boring parts of the *Life* for laymen are those where Boswell, a practising advocate who had very little law, consults Johnson on his cases: on at least eight occasions Johnson wrote or dictated long and learned views. McAdam's most important addition to the canon of Johnson's writings is his discovery that he had actually collaborated in the lectures of his friend Robert Chambers, Vinerian Professor of Law at Oxford and later an Indian judge. Chambers had been appointed to his chair in 1762, but like many academics of his time did not give any lectures for some years; finding himself under pressure to fulfil his obligations and unable to do so, he called for Johnson's help. Johnson evidently dictated part of the lectures in 1766, and Chambers was able to start giving them in the following year. Johnson's hand has been detected in the style, wide range of topics, and philosophical approach, as in the Parliamentary Debates; and like the prefaces and sermons they are an example of Johnson's warm, even careless, generosity in putting his talents at the disposal of his friends. Johnson's legal interests and practical bias set him apart from most other literary moralists, since he was not content with talking about good and evil in the abstract. Showing a low opinion of human nature as well as great sympathy for human suffering, he saw the law, like politics, as a means of alleviating the miseries of the world. His remarks on legal reform have as great a weight of knowledge as of feeling behind them.

In the *Rambler* (142 and 148) he discusses the inequality of the poor before the law, at a time when few had thought of suggesting free legal aid. In the *Idler* (23 and 38) he attacks another scandal of the age, the position of debtors. It should be remembered that a creditor had the power to send his debtor to prison, and this could mean a life sentence. A century before Dickens, Johnson pities the cry of 'remember the poor Debtors': at this time twenty thousand debtors were in prison.

> The wisdom and justice of the English laws are, by Englishmen at least, loudly celebrated; but scarcely the most zealous admirers of our Institutions can think that law wise, which, when men are capable of work, obliges them to beg; or just, which exposes the liberty of one to the passions of another. . . . The confinement, therefore, of any man in the sloth and darkness of a prison, is a loss to the nation, and no gain to the Creditor. For of the multitudes who are pining in those cells of misery, a very small part is suspected of any fraudulent act by which they retain what belongs to others. The rest are imprisoned by the wantonness of pride, the malignity of revenge, or the acrimony of disappointed expectation.

His most important contribution, however, was to the reform of the English criminal law, as it related to capital punishment. The background to this, which has been given a classic description by Leon Radzinowicz in *A History of English Criminal Law*, is the most shocking aspect of Johnson's age. Crime was continuously on the increase, from a variety of causes, including the lack of any effective police force. The only way of coping with crime that the legislature could think of was to increase the deterrents, and that meant increasing the number of capital offences, from about fifty at the beginning to over two hundred at the end of the eighteenth century. The crimes that incurred the death penalty included not only murder (which was never very common), but rape, sodomy, arson, stealing livestock or goods worth 40*s*., being in the company of gipsies, and as we shall see forgery. The Waltham Black Act, passed in 1722 to stop an outbreak of poaching, alone added dozens of new capital crimes to the statute book. By no means all the criminals who were tried or sentenced to death were actually executed: the form of criminal procedure was very liberal; witnesses would refuse to testify, and juries to convict, when conviction could only mean death, or they deliberately undervalued stolen goods to save a petty thief from the gallows. The Royal Prerogative of Mercy was often used, and death sentences commuted to transportation or imprisonment. There were nevertheless a horrifying number of executions: 'During the twenty years from 1750 to 1769, 909 offenders were capitally convicted, of whom 551 were executed, for crimes committed in London and Middlesex only. In the year 1770 alone, 91 capital verdicts were given and 49 offenders put to death.' (Radzinowicz, p. 426.) Almost all these sentences were for offences against property, not the person; and apparently nine out of ten of the executed were under twenty-one. Even children of eight were sentenced to death and boys of fourteen hanged, and a few wretched women were burned for coining. Apart from being grossly inhumane, the system was inefficient, since so many criminals escaped to swell the huge army of footpads and highwaymen. Yet Johnson's was the first and for many years the only voice to be raised against it. In the *Rambler* 114 (1751) he made a logical and moving case for the abolition of the death penalty for crimes against property.

> To equate robbery with murder is to reduce murder to robbery, to confound in common minds the gradations of iniquity, and incite the commission of a greater crime to prevent the detection of a less. If only murder were punished with death, very few robbers would stain their hands in blood; and when by the last act of cruelty no new danger is incurred, and greater security may be obtained, upon what principle shall we bid them forbear?

He knew that his proposals were revolutionary: 'This scheme of invigorating the laws by relaxation, and extirpating wickedness by lenity, is so remote from common practice, that I might reasonably fear to expose it to the public. . . .' In fact, there was little progress in reform until the eighteen-twenties; but this *Rambler* essay was quoted by the Attorney-General in the debate of 1832, to good effect.

In February 1777 Johnson intervened vigorously in the case of Dr Dodd. The Rev. William Dodd was a fashionable preacher and essayist and had been tutor to Lord Chesterfield's son; having got into debt through extravagance, he forged his old pupil's name on a bond for £4,300 and was at once caught. Although he confessed his guilt and made full restitution, the jury could do nothing but find him guilty, and that meant a death sentence. Johnson took up the case, although he hardly knew Dodd and had a low opinion of his writings and morals: although he did not say so, it must have been because he thought that the penalty for forgery was irrationally severe, and that in this instance it would be judicial murder. 'Be comforted,' he wrote to Dodd, 'your crime, morally or religiously considered, has no very deep dye of turpitude. It corrupted no man's principles: it attacked no man's life. It involved only a temporary and reparable injury.' Johnson wrote a speech for Dodd to deliver at his trial, and then took the lead in a mass campaign to obtain a reprieve. He drafted a number of petitions, which were signed by thousands of people; wrote letters for Dodd and on his behalf; and, to create a good impression of Dodd's character, even composed a sermon for him to deliver to his 'unhappy Brethren' in Newgate. Johnson was judicious as well as warm-hearted: he was anxious to show that the majesty of justice would be maintained if Dodd received only transportation, as appears from the *Observations* he sent to the newspapers and the letter he wrote to the Secretary of War:

> The supreme power has, in all ages, paid some attention to the voice of the people; and that voice does not least deserve to be heard when it calls out for mercy. There is now a very general desire that Dodd's life should be spared. More is not desired; and, perhaps, this is not too much to be granted.

Popular sympathy for Dodd was intense, and everything depended on the King. But George III had the previous year refused to pardon the Perreau brothers for forgery (they had been convicted on the evidence of their accomplice Mrs Rudd, who later became Boswell's mistress); and he may have thought it would be weak and inconsistent to give way over Dodd. There was no pardon, and in June Dodd was duly hanged at Tyburn before a crowd of record size.

It must not be thought, however, that Johnson was a sentimental opponent of public executions. The eighteenth century was the heroic age of the criminal. Jack Shepherd and Jonathan Wild became heroes of the broadsheets, and were reflected in literature by the gallant Captain Macheath of the *Beggar's Opera*, as potent and obsessive a symbol as the Western outlaw of today—as can be seen from Boswell's modelling himself on Macheath in the *London Journal*. The hanging at Tyburn, where the hero met his end with manly fortitude, had a dramatic ritual. There was a public holiday, a solemn procession of the condemned man and his mourners from Newgate through the crowded streets (when Dodd passed, we are told, 'ten thousand hats swept from ten thousand heads'), a collection raised for the bereaved family, a short and game speech on the scaffold and a leave-taking of old friends, who would sometimes help the hangman to ensure a quick death. There is no evidence that Johnson ever attended these spectacles, although Boswell often did. But Johnson in his old age was indignant when there was talk of abolishing the traditional ritual: 'the public was gratified by a procession; the criminal was supported by it. Why is all this to be swept away?' We must suppose that this was an irritable lapse on the part of one whose humanity rarely slumbered, and whose sympathy and compassion were almost unbounded.

19 Johnson in his Hebridean costume

Chapter 7

JOHNSON THE CRITIC

7 JOHNSON THE CRITIC

1777–1781

Before Dodd was in his grave, Johnson was hard at work on *The Lives of the Poets*. The story of the next four years, the last happy and creative period of his life, is soon told. For most of the time he stayed with the Thrales at Southwark and Streatham, engaged in research and writing. At week-ends and when the Thrales were away, he conscientiously returned to his house and 'family' in Bolt Court; he made only a few short trips to Lichfield, Brighton, or other places not far afield. Mrs Thrale helped him with the *Lives*, acting as amanuensis and proof-corrector, and Boswell, whom he saw every year except 1780, was also useful. Johnson lived in ever greater intimacy with and dependence on the Thrales, giving advice when the brewery again got into difficulties, supervising the children's education, and, whenever they were away from home, writing long letters to Mrs Thrale. In 1779 Henry Thrale had a stroke, brought on by gross and wilful over-eating: Johnson, in despair about the consequences for his friend and for himself, wrote to Mrs Thrale with deep feeling: 'There is nobody left for me to care about but you and my master.' Thrale recovered, but was too feeble to have any hope of success in the election of 1780, at which Johnson again loyally exerted himself. In 1781 the Thrales, hoping to move into fashionable society, took a new house in Grosvenor Square. Here too Johnson had a room kept for him; but there were to be few days left for the old life with his 'master' and 'mistress'.

The *Lives* made good progress. In 1779 the first four volumes were published, but there was some delay before Johnson began writing his masterpiece, the *Life* of Pope. There are perhaps signs of hurry towards the end of the series, reflected in the impatience he showed towards the last two poets, Gray and Lyttelton. The publication of these two essays started a serious quarrel with Mrs Montagu and the Blue-Stocking circle, who thought (rightly about Gray) that Johnson had been insensitive and disrespectful. The work was finished in March 1781 and the last six volumes published in May. Apart from revision of the *Lives* and one great poem, Johnson's career as a writer was over.

The *Lives* are prefaces to a curious collection of poets, chosen by the booksellers and not by Johnson, who made only a few changes in the proposed list, agreeing to the omission of his dear friend Goldsmith but insisting on that of the profligate and radical Churchill. Of the fifty writers only about thirty get into modern anthologies or histories; only five are taken from English poetry before the Restoration; and the prefaces vary greatly in length and interest. The only long ones, apart from the reprinted life of Savage, are those of Cowley, Milton, Dryden, Addison, Swift, Pope, and Young; Pope and Dryden make up complete books on their own, while some of the minor writers get only a few hundred words. A large part of the work is purely biographical, and here Johnson worked harder than is usually thought. Apart from the standard works he used a good deal of private information in his research. He may have been irritated by Boswell's insistence that he should consult Lord Marchmont on Pope, exclaiming, 'if it rained knowledge I'd hold out my hand; but I would not give myself the trouble to go in quest of it'; but he did in fact wait upon Marchmont, as well as using Spence's record of Pope's talk, in manuscript, and other first-hand sources. The result is in each case almost entirely successful, accurate, and thorough. If he did not create a new method of biography, he used his immense knowledge of the world and his intuitive grasp of character to splendid effect. The charm of the essays comes from the relaxed, confident style and the witty apothegms about manners and morals: 'Large offers and sturdy rejections are among the most common topics of falsehood' and 'No man sympathizes with the sorrows of vanity' show Johnson's kindly and uncynical irony. There are places where he goes wrong, and from significant causes. It has been shown that the 'Life of Swift' is full of slight distortions and hostile interpretations of the facts: this was because he saw himself as only too like Swift in imaginative power and instability; fearing madness as his own likely fate, he came to dislike Swift so much that fairness was impossible. Johnson's needling of Gray is the result not only of his views about poetry but also of the class feeling that keeps cropping up in English literary criticism: Gray was an Etonian, a friend of Horace Walpole, 'effeminate' and excessively refined, and therefore could expect no mercy.

Although Johnson read much in the field of biography, he did not, we can be sure, trouble to re-read any of the poetry he criticized. What he liked, he knew by heart; what he did not, he had long ago consigned to limbo. His fantastic memory, equalled only by a few prodigies like Macaulay and James Joyce, held thousands of lines of Pope and Dryden in instant readiness for quotation. If he quotes only two and a half lines of *Paradise Lost*, it is because he has not loved it well enough to learn it; as he frankly admits, it 'is one of the books which the reader admires and lays down, and forgets to take up again'. He would now and then turn to editions of minor writers to refresh his memory before writing a sentence or two of practical criticism. But he had done little exploratory reading in the English poets since preparing the *Dictionary*. His criticism is the product of fifty years of meditation on the library he carried in his head. Nor did he read everything that other critics had written. Since, however, he needed controversy to sharpen his thought, he kept an eye on a few of the critics and countered their arguments. Hilles has shown that much of the 'Life of Pope' consists of a dialogue with one or other of his predecessors, Ruffhead and Joseph Warton, in which the opponent's name is not mentioned. The dialectic leads up to the pugnacious question at the end: 'If Pope be not a poet, where is poetry to be found?' Johnson was writing for victory.

The *Lives of the Poets* completes the corpus of Johnson's literary criticism, which must be viewed as a whole. Beginning with his notes in the translation of Crousaz (1739), it includes essays in the *Rambler* and *Idler*, parts of *Rasselas*, the preface and notes to his edition of Shakespeare, and of course many of the conversations recorded by Boswell. In all this there is great consistency of principle and opinion, and not much development: as he grew older, Johnson grew wiser but did not change his mind about essentials. A survivor from the great days of Queen Anne and early Georgian literature, the true Augustan Age, he had become, by the time that the *Lives* was published, quite out of sympathy with new fashions in poetry and in critical theory. What he admired most was the peculiar combination of tough realism and formal elegance developed by the great Tory satirists. He shared their pessimistic view of humanity: 'we are to consider mankind, not as we wish them but as we find them, frequently corrupt and always fallible', he had written in the *Parliamentary Debates*, in the spirit of Pope or Swift. He shared their notion of how poetry could achieve its moral purpose: the object of writing was to chastise vice and folly by the sharp delineation of contemporary fools and knaves. He was totally devoted to the traditional medium of verse satire, the balanced end-stopped couplet, invented by Denham and Waller, improved by Dryden and perfected by Pope. For the music of this couplet his ear was exquisite, and except for Goldsmith he was himself the only eighteenth-century poet to approach at all closely the cadences of his masters. He also admired the short-lined Restoration quatrain, and used it to perfection in 'A Short Song of Congratulation', a re-creation of the sardonic Restoration outlook and incidentally the starting-point of Housman's quatrains.

Long-expected one and twenty
Ling'ring year at last is flown,
Pomp and Pleasure, Pride and Plenty
Great Sir John, are all your own.

. . .

Wealth, Sir John, was made to wander
Let it wander as it will;
See the Jockey, see the Pander,
Bid them come, and take their fill.

. . .

If the Guardian or the Mother,
Tell the woes of wilful waste,
Scorn their counsel and their pother,
You can hang or drown at last.

20 Johnson's house in Bolt Court
Engraved from a drawing by J. T. Smith

21 The Westminster Abbey portrait: a bust by Joseph Nollekens

To nearly all other kinds of verse-music he was tone-deaf, whether to Milton's blank verse or Thomson's imitations of it or Gray's experiments in the *Odes*. His objections to contemporary verse were not of course merely metrical. He disliked the changes in poetic thought and style which had begun even in Pope's lifetime; everything, in fact, that was affected by the cult of 'Sensibility'.

The new trend, which for want of a better name has to be called Pre-Romanticism, began early in Johnson's lifetime. The Earl of Shaftesbury's *Characteristics*, published in 1711, is shallow as philosophy and bombastic in style, but was nevertheless one of the most influential books of the century. Shaftesbury publicized the notion of the man of feeling, inspired by benevolence towards his fellow-creatures, who vibrates sympathetically before wild nature. He helped to strengthen the feeling that the primitive was preferable to the civilized, the natural to the artificial, the irregular to the orderly. These ideas were spread by the first popularizer Addison, and were taken up enthusiastically by the new school of landscape gardeners, and by the poets. James Thomson's *Seasons*, which Johnson thought could be improved by leaving out every other line, presented Shaftesburian benevolence and nature-worship in Miltonic blank verse; and Thomson was followed by Akenside, who anticipates Wordsworth in so many ways though not in poetical greatness. The search for the primitive led the poets into new territory. In the present, the primitive meant both the noble savages discovered by explorers in the South Seas and America, and the virtuous peasantry of Britain. But the past offered even more imaginative possibilities: sympathy for the Middle Ages encouraged the Gothic Revival in the poetry of Gray and the Wartons as well as in architecture. Gray's *Bard* (1757) had a signal effect on the new taste for the 'sublime' and the 'picturesque'; and it inspired James Macpherson to fabricate his notorious 'Ossian', the first part of which came out in 1762. Bishop Percy's *Reliques*, published three years later, started a new fashion in romantic ballads and folk-lore; while the 'young whelp' Chatterton manufactured a complete set of medieval poems, in an unsuccessful attempt to outbid even 'Ossian'.

To all this Johnson was strongly opposed. His scholarly instincts led him to admire the researches of Percy and others into the past; but that a poet should try to form a new style by imitating ballads struck him as ridiculous. He showed his contempt of the Gothic fashion in a parody of Thomas Warton:

Hermit hoar, in solemn cell,
Wearing out life's evening gray:
Smite thy bosom, sage, and tell,
What is bliss? and which the way?

Thus I spoke; and speaking sigh'd;
—Scarce repress'd the starting tear;—
When the smiling sage reply'd—
—Come, my lad, and drink some beer.

This explains Johnson's coldness to everything of Gray's except the *Elegy*; while his hostility to Macpherson's 'Ossian' led to an open explosion. With his back turned on the most interesting developments of the age, he found only one consolation in poetry after Goldsmith's death: he lived long enough to discover, praise, and encourage Crabbe, who was in some ways his true successor and who survived him by fifty years.

Johnson did not undertake the literary criticism of much besides poetry, even in conversation. As an unsuccessful dramatist himself, he did not show much interest in the living theatre. Despite his close association with Garrick, he saw Shakespeare as a creator of poetic fiction rather than as man of the theatre. He knew Restoration tragedy well—indeed *Irene* is an exercise in that obsolete mode—but took little trouble to keep up with later drama. He was latterly too deaf to enjoy the playhouse, and where new productions were concerned his was no great loss. With the exception of Goldsmith's and Sheridan's, which he admired, eighteenth-century comedy was clogged with sentimentality: it would seem to be a law of literary history that comedy is hardly possible without the kind of Elizabethan or Restoration freedom and irreverence that puritans have always deplored. If Johnson took a fairly liberal view of comedy, he disliked the irreverence of Henry Fielding, whom he lost no chance of unfairly disparaging—and Sterne was to him even worse. Johnson, like all other critics of his day, failed to take the novel seriously as a major art form. But to his eternal credit he spoke, if he would not write, in praise of his old friend Richardson, whose masterpieces *Pamela* and *Clarissa* he claimed to be incomparable for their 'knowledge of the heart'. Apart from Richardson he admired only the novels of his clever friend Fanny Burney. The essay was to him a more serious matter than the novel. If in Johnson's lifetime poetry developed far and fast, the essay tradition, as established by Addison, remained surprisingly static: of the thousands of eighteenth-century essays, including Johnson's own, there are very few that depart from the pattern of moral comment and gentle satire. The personal essay, invented by Montaigne to describe the author's mind in the act of thinking, was not used as a form again until the early nineteenth century; and no doubt Johnson's example helped to maintain the Addisonian stereotype. Of the other kinds of eighteenth-century literature which are read today, Johnson says comparatively little. The greatest prose artist of his contemporaries was Gibbon; but Boswell is so bitter about Gibbon for personal reasons that it is impossible to find out what Johnson really felt about him. (Gibbon on the other hand disliked and feared Johnson, as is evident from some of the footnotes to the *Decline and Fall.*) Burke was to Johnson the outstanding mind of the age, but he makes no comment on Burke's work as literature. Finally, Johnson largely ignored the literary critics of his age, and with some justice.

The business of the critic is primarily to number the streaks of the tulip. He must begin with accurate observation and description of the work he is writing about, and these can only come from love: he must achieve the kind of affectionate intimacy which will allow him to *see* his subject clearly. Next he must be a master of the background to his subject. Since literature is of its essence an impure art, and may include almost anything in its scope, the critic must be learned in all the relevant fields, which are social history, philosophy, and the literature of other cultures. Thirdly, the critic must possess good judgment. This means the ability to say what is good and bad about a work of art, and to estimate its value relative to other works, without being influenced by gross prejudices or irrelevant considerations. Fourthly, if criticism is to take its place among the intellectual disciplines, the critic must be able to make significant generalizations. The greatest literary criticism, like that of Aristotle and Coleridge, is signalized by its power to produce theories; theories which cannot offer the degree of verifiability required of the mathematical sciences, but which are analogous to those of history and the social sciences. By raising the discussion to a high enough level of abstraction, criticism can hope to show what are the basic qualities of good literature.

In the first three of these respects Johnson was by far the greatest critic of his century and has rarely been surpassed since. When he dealt with authors whom he loved, like Shakespeare and Pope, he was the acutest of observers, illuminating his subjects by his sympathetic insight and knowledge of detail. As a literary scholar he had a few limitations, as in his grasp of social and intellectual history, which was not as firm perhaps as he wished a Shakespearian scholar's to be; but against that he had his unparalleled knowledge of the English language, and his massive classical scholarship. In the third place, his judgment, based on integrity and common sense, was as fair as any man's can be: this was never shown more clearly than in his considered opinion of Milton, whose politics he execrated but whose epic he praised in words of appropriate respect. It was only in literary theory that Johnson shared the defects of his age, or transcended them imperfectly. He was the last great exponent of the neoclassical tradition, which had lasted for two thousand years; and since the theory of this tradition is alien to modern readers, it is necessary to look at it in a little detail before discussing Johnson's peculiar deviations from it.

The origin of neoclassicism lies not in Aristotle, who was largely misunderstood by his followers, but in Horace's *Ars Poetica.* This poem consists of about thirty critical precepts strung together with great skill and in a highly quotable form; and of these the chief three are the pre-eminence of moral poetry, the proper use of poetic models, and the importance of careful art. The first principle is expressed in two famous tags: wisdom (which implies morality) is the source of good writing, and poetry should instruct as well as delight. This emphasis on the moral function of poetry, a perversion of Aristotle's views, was repeated by every critic from the Renaissance up to the Romantic Age. It had an especial appeal to Johnson, since he was always preoccupied with the moral problems presented by living, and believed that it was always a writer's duty to make the world better. The principle is presented in its clearest form in the *Life* of Milton: all poetry must instruct, epic poetry instructs in the highest virtues, therefore the epic is the best form of poetry:

> By the general consent of criticks, the first praise of genius is due to the writer of an epick poem, as it requires an assemblage of all the powers which are singly sufficient for other compositions. Poetry is the art of uniting pleasure with truth, by calling imagination to the help of reason. Epick poetry undertakes to teach the most important truths by the most pleasing precepts, and therefore relates some great event in the most affecting manner.

Poetry, then, presents truths, but what kind of truths? On the basis of a traditional misunderstanding of Aristotle's statement that poetry deals with universals, Johnson elaborated his own doctrine of the 'General' as opposed to the 'Particular'. In some places he seems to think of poetic truths as the abstract precepts of morality, abstract because 'the most useful truths are always universal and unconnected with accidents or customs' (*Idler* 66). The poet, says Imlac in Chapter X of *Rasselas*, 'must consider right and wrong in their abstracted and invariable state; he must disregard present laws and opinions, and rise to general and transcendental truths, which will always be the same'. This would seem to imply that there is nothing really new for a poet to say. Johnson in fact makes the melancholy reflection in his *Life* of Dryden that 'whatever can happen to man has happened so often, that little remains for fancy or invention'; in that case, all a poet can do is to dress up the permanent truths in persuasive and rhetorical language: all literature is the same sermon about good and evil, expressed in varied and picturesque terms only to hold the readers' attention. Fortunately, as we shall see, Johnson departed on the most important occasions from this crippling doctrine.

The second principle of neoclassicism advocated the use of poetic models: the poet must be faithful to the traditional forms and genres, producing a tragedy or a comedy or an epic in accordance with the plans laid down by the Greeks and by their imitators in Latin. This theory too was dear to Johnson: his two great satires follow Juvenal's models closely, just as his essays are faithful to the Addisonian tradition. In strict classical theory, there is a proper subject-matter and style for each genre: tragedy is about princes and is written in high style, comedy about the lower orders and in low style. This involves the notion of 'decorum', which insists that there is only one way of presenting any aspect of life: in speech and action princes must be princely, and peasants peasantlike, just as they ought to be in the real world. Literature is the dignified expression of traditional values, and by preserving the ancient forms acts as a civilizing force.

By the importance of careful art, which is the third canon, a neoclassical critic meant that technique was more important than inspiration. Keep your poem for nine years, says Horace, applying the file to it all the time until it has attained to polished perfection. The metaphor is from craftsmanship: the poet is not a visionary seer or an ecstatic bard but a good workman. This too accords with Johnson's views. He granted that there was something called 'imagination' with which a poet must be endowed; but to him the writing of poetry involved mainly the conscientious labour of revising. 'Composition is, for the most part, an effort of slow diligence and steady perseverance' (*Adventurer* 138). Hence his irritation with poor Gray's dependence on the visitation of his Muse: 'he had a notion not very peculiar, that he could not write but at certain times, or at happy moments; a fantastick foppery, to which my kindness for a man of learning and of virtue wishes him to have been superior'.

In his criticism Johnson violated each of these three canons in turn, as if against his will and impelled by something stronger than his respect for authority. In each case the stumbling-block was Shakespeare. First, Shakespeare 'seems to write without any moral purpose' and 'makes no just distribution of good or evil, nor is always careful to shew in the virtuous a disapprobation of the wicked'. So much for the ethical content of poetry; and Shakespeare is no more to be trusted when it comes to preserving the traditional forms; his plays 'are not in the rigorous and critical sense either tragedies or comedies, but compositions of a distinct kind'. Thirdly, Shakespeare was notoriously careless about revising:

> The plots are often so loosely formed, that a very slight consideration may improve them, and so carelessly pursued, that he seems not always fully to comprehend his own design. . . . In many of his plays the latter part is evidently neglected. When he found himself near the end of his work and in view of his reward, he shortened the labour to snatch the profit.

Johnson nevertheless is saying that none of these defects really matters in the assessment of Shakespeare's genius. What does matter to him, whenever he considers essentials, is truth to nature. 'Nothing can please many, and please long, but just representations of general nature . . . the mind can only repose on the stability of truth'; and Shakespeare 'is above all writers, at least above all modern writers, the poet of nature'. This is in fact a naturalistic position, which Johnson always invokes whenever the canons of neoclassical criticism begin to constrain him. The word 'nature' is of course notorious for having a wide range of meaning—and especially during the eighteenth century, when it could cover almost anything—but Johnson's use of this key word is fairly consistent. The meaning he usually gives to it is something like 'the eternal verities of human existence', but sometimes he will narrow it to 'the basic laws of human behaviour'. Human nature is to Johnson 'always the same', and 'poetry has to do rather with the passions of men, which are uniform, than their customs, which are changeable'. There is to him no opposition between nature in this sense and art: he does not use the word 'artificial' in a pejorative sense, and always ridicules Rousseauistic sentiments and calls to go 'back to nature'. For, if 'a just representation of things really existing and actions really performed' is what is required of a writer if you are to call him 'natural', then there can be no such opposition, 'nature being, in this sense, only the best effect of art'. It is the poet's task, then, to reveal how the human mind works, and to create a kind of natural science of the emotions and of the conscience. (The analogy with science would not have displeased Johnson.) Poetry and poetic drama must hold up a 'faithful mirrour' of nature, and in this respect Shakespeare is supreme:

> His characters are not modified by the customs of particular places, unpractised by the rest of the world; by the peculiarities of studies or professions, which can operate but upon small numbers; or by the accidents of transient fashions or temporary opinions; they are the genuine progeny of common humanity, such as the world will always supply, and observation will always find. His persons act and speak by the influence of those general passions and principles by which all minds are agitated, and the whole system of life is continued in motion. In the writings of other poets a character is too often an individual; in those of *Shakespeare* it is commonly a species.

Johnson's criticism, then, is based on two conflicting sets of principles. When he writes about Milton's epic or Pope's couplets, he thinks like a neoclassical critic, and this is in conformity with his Anglican and High Tory views: literature is the guardian of civilization, poetry is the expression of harmony and dignity, and the traditional order is all-important. But when he writes about Shakespeare, his profoundest philosophical convictions come to the fore: he is realist, empirical and scientific. What now matters most is that literature should give a true account of objective reality, and that means primarily of human nature. With such an approach, Johnson would probably have given the highest praise to the great Russian and English novelists of the nineteenth century; it is significant that he singles out Richardson's novels for their insight into the passions. Whenever in his discussions a point is reached where neoclassical and realist principles begin to clash, it is always the latter that prevail. Thus, he rejects the traditional doctrine of the Unities, which insists that the action of a play be confined to one time and place, with a brisk appeal to common sense. 'The spectators are always in their senses, and know, from the first act to the last, that the stage is only a stage, and that the players are only players.' He rejects the heroic-erotic tradition of seventeenth-century drama, because the 'hero', motivated only by honour and love, is an imaginary class of being, and because passionate love is not very important in real life. In the preface he writes that '*Shakespeare* has no heroes; his scenes are occupied only by men, who act and speak as the reader thinks that he should himself have spoken or acted on the same occasion'; and he returns to the attack on 'love' and the Heroic Play in his *Life* of Dryden: 'by admitting the romantick omnipotence of Love, he has recommended as laudable and worthy of imitation that conduct which, through all ages, the good have censured as vitious, and the bad despised as foolish'. He dismisses Pope's *Unfortunate Lady* as 'the amorous fury of a raving girl'.

In other ways his criticism is realist. He keeps his eye firmly on the text, and works through it like an editor or a publisher's reader: from his long experience as a practical journalist, he knows that almost everything, except short passages of poetry, can be improved in argument or polish; being himself a generous reviser of other men's work, he convinces you that he could supply the improvement if required. This practical approach may seem to lack the reverence due from a mere critic to genius (and Johnson is sadly irreverent when it comes to 'Lycidas' or Donne), but it conveys a sense of intimacy for which Johnson is unsurpassed. Next, Johnson is concerned with imparting solid information about literature. It is striking that the *Lives of the Poets* is still read keenly today, not only by pious Johnsonians but by ordinary students of literature: this is because Johnson tells them more in a short space than any other critic. He tells them what the poets were writing about: he goes straight to the plot of a play, and to the characters as they relate to the plot. The speed with which he reaches the central core is never better shown than in his comments on *Henry IV*. These have been praised by Dover Wilson as revealing the finest insight of all criticism into Shakespeare's intentions, especially as regards the political and moral meaning of the play; free from sentimentality, they yet avoid the priggishness of many scholars who cannot respond to Falstaff's humanity as magnificently as this:

> But *Falstaff* unimitated, unimitable *Falstaff*, how shall I describe thee? Thou compound of sense and vice; of sense which may be admired but not esteemed, of vice which may be despised, but hardly detested. . . . Yet the man thus corrupt, thus despicable, makes himself necessary to the prince that despises him, by the most pleasing of all qualities, perpetual gaiety, by an unfailing power of exciting laughter, which is the more freely indulged, as his wit is not of the splendid or ambitious kind, but consists in easy escapes and sallies of levity, which make sport but raise no envy.

Johnson is also a realist in making his literary criticism biographical. Literature to him is not an autonomous realm nor is poetry a pure artefact. Poems are written by living men, in real social and historical settings. No one has yet proved logically that biographical information is necessary to criticism, nor conversely that any of it may be irrelevant. Johnson had doubts about the value of every biographical item: 'I know not well what Advantage Posterity can receive from the only Circumstance by which Tickell has distinguished *Addison* from the Rest of Mankind, the Irregularity of his Pulse' (though even this may tell us that Addison died of heart disease). But he is usually uninhibited about putting down a wealth of detail: Pope 'never drank tea without a stratagem', Dryden's magisterial arm-chair at Will's Coffee House which 'in the winter had a settled and prescriptive place by the fire, was in the summer placed in the balcony', and so on. Such things prove nothing about poetry, but they reveal the man and thereby the poet. Johnson's short lives are the model for Boswell's concept of 'total' biography. Johnson has the ability to relate everything to his own experience of life, and to identify himself closely with the men he writes about, sharing their problems and emotions. He achieved perfection in his early life of Savage, and came near to it again in parts of his *Life* of Swift. As a whole, this *Life* is incomplete and unfair; but, as Krutch says, the horror of Swift's last days has never 'been presented more simply or more impressively': Johnson, always afraid of madness and now aware of the end of his career, re-creates Swift's situation in an outburst of imaginative intensity.

> Having thus excluded conversation, and desisted from study, he had neither business nor amusement; for, having by some ridiculous resolution, or mad vow, determined never to wear spectacles, he could make little use of books in his later years; his ideas, therefore, being neither renovated by discourse, nor increased by reading, wore gradually away, and left his mind vacant to the vexations of the hour, till, at last, his anger was heightened into madness. . . . A short interval of reason ensuing, in which he knew his physician and his family, gave hopes for his recovery; but in a few days he sunk into a lethargick stupidity, motionless, heedless, and speechless. But it is said, that, after a year of total silence, when his housekeeper, on the 30th of November, told him that the usual bonfires and illuminations were preparing to celebrate his birthday, he answered, 'It is all folly; they had better let it alone.'

If a man lives on into the seventies, his last memorable experience will usually be the death of his friends and contemporaries. To the sturdy and malicious this may be a cause of self-congratulation; but Johnson both cared deeply for others and feared his own extinction. In 1779 David Garrick died, as Johnson was writing a tribute to their common friend of Lichfield days, Gilbert Walmsley:

> At this man's table I enjoyed many chearful and instructive hours, with companions such as are not often found; with one who has lengthened, and one who has gladdened life; with Dr. James, whose skill in physick will be long remembered; and with David Garrick, whom I hoped to have gratified with this character of our common friend; but what are the hopes of man! I am disappointed by that stroke of death, which has eclipsed the gaiety of nations, and impoverished the publick stock of harmless pleasure.

In the following year Topham Beauclerk died, and in 1781, while the last of the *Lives* were in proof, fell the worst stroke of all. On 4th April, Henry Thrale, deaf to Johnson's warnings about gluttony, died of his second stroke. It is hardly possible to exaggerate what this loss meant to Johnson, who wrote in his Good Friday meditation: 'I felt almost the last flutter of his pulse, and looked for the last time upon the face that for fifteen years had never been turned upon me but with respect or benignity.' Whatever Johnson's emotional relationship with Mrs Thrale may have been, and it was certainly profound, it must not be assumed that Henry Thrale meant any less to him. Thrale had been his 'Master', his manners and hospitality had been perfect, and his financial and political troubles had been Johnson's own concern. Despite his coolness and egocentricity, there had been a generosity and frankness in Thrale, to which Johnson had responded with warmth and gratitude. When, two years later, he published 'On the Death of Dr. Robert Levet', it was not only of his eccentric friend, the silent and grimy quack physician, that he was thinking. The poem is about all his dead friends, and first among them Henry Thrale, for it was he who had suffered the 'cold gradations of decay'.

Condemn'd to hope's delusive mine,
As on we toil from day to day,
By sudden blasts, or slow decline,
Our social comforts drop away.

Well tried through many a varying year,
See LEVET to the grave descend;
Officious, innocent, sincere,
Of ev'ry friendless name the friend.

Yet still he fills affection's eye,
Obscurely wise, and coarsely kind;
Nor, letter'd arrogance, deny
Thy praise to merit unrefin'd.

. . .

His virtues walk'd their narrow round,
Nor made a pause, nor left a void;
And sure th' Eternal Master found
The single talent well employ'd.

The busy day, the peaceful night,
Unfelt, uncounted, glided by;
His frame was firm, his powers were bright,
Tho' now his eightieth year was nigh.

Then with no throbbing fiery pain,
No cold gradations of decay,
Death broke at once the vital chain,
And forc'd his soul the nearest way.

Chapter 8

WISDOM

8 WISDOM

1781–1784

JOHNSON was 'willing to speak favourably of his own age, and, indeed, maintained its superiority in every respect, except in its reverence for government'. There was, however, little to be said in favour of the early 'eighties. The political situation had deteriorated while Johnson was finishing the *Lives*, as the American war went from disaster to disaster, thanks to the incompetent leadership of Lord North and the stubbornness of the King. The Gordon Riots of 1780, which Johnson reported calmly enough to Mrs Thrale, were not revolutionary but anti-Catholic, but they were a symptom of the distress caused by the war, and of a general 'lack of reverence' for government. The mob was able to do an appalling amount of damage because the government was so weak, having lost the confidence of the Commons. Dunning's motion in the same year made Boswell ask if public affairs really vexed no man:

> Have you not been vexed by all the turbulence of this reign, and by that absurd vote of the House of Commons, 'That the influence of the Crown has increased, is increasing, and ought to be diminished'? JOHNSON: 'Sir, I have never slept an hour less, nor eat an ounce less meat. I would have knocked 'em on the head, to be sure; but I was not vexed.' [Boswell improved this into 'knocked the factious dogs'.]

Outside Parliament a radical movement was growing, which was sympathetic to American independence and was concerned with reform of the suffrage. This movement had the sympathy of vigorous entrepreneurs like Josiah Wedgwood, and came to influence even the professional politicians, among them Johnson's friends Burke and Charles James Fox. In the confusion after the peace with America and the fall of North in 1782, when groups of Whigs fought for power with George III, Johnson's sympathies were curiously divided.

> I asked him [wrote Boswell] if it was true as reported, that he said lately, 'I am for the King against Fox; but I am for Fox against Pitt.' JOHNSON: 'Yes, Sir; the King is my master; but I do not know Pitt; and Fox is my friend.' He went on to pay tribute to that 'most extraordinary man' Fox, who was now a member of the Club: '. . . here is a man . . . who has divided the kingdom with Caesar',

referring to Fox's attempt in 1783 to break the power of the Crown in politics. George III held on firmly and found an opportunity to break the Whigs over the East India Bill; in December 1783 he brought his supporter, young William Pitt, to power, whose majority was secured by the General Election of March 1784—the last Prime Minister of Johnson's lifetime. Boswell rightly notes that Johnson 'lived to see the Crown at last recover its just influence', but not that he showed much rejoicing.

The American war affected the country's economy even more harmfully than its politics. Exports and imports dropped steeply from their peak in the early 'seventies to a point little higher than that of forty years earlier. 1780 and '81 were years of general depression in trade and industry; the consumption of liquor and other indices of prosperity showed a sharp decline, and there is evidence of hard times among the people. An improvement began in 1782, although it was offset at first by the bad harvests of this and the following years, which were followed by high prices and food riots. Thereafter the effect of the peace was surprisingly tonic: the cost of maintaining huge armed forces was no longer a burden, the world's markets were open, and with the loss of America English merchants and entrepreneurs turned to their own resources, which were now very great. The technical progress and capital investment of the last twenty years suddenly caused an economic explosion, as described by T. S. Ashton:

After 1782 almost every statistical series of production shows a sharp upward turn. More than half the growth in the shipment of coal and the mining of copper, more than three-quarters of the increase of broadcloths, four-fifths of that of printed cloth, and nine-tenths of the exports of cotton goods were concentrated in the last eighteen years of the eighteenth century.[1]

The population began to expand rapidly, but it would seem that the standard of living of the masses also rose, as can be judged from the figures for tea, calico, and other luxuries of the poor. These were years of great technical improvement. The agricultural revolution and the enclosures continued, and the English landscape was transformed by creative planning. The new turnpike roads made travel much easier, and even more was done in the development of canals. The Irish navvy (derived from 'navigation', Johnson's word for canal) in his thousands tore up the countryside and laid 3,000 miles of canal, between the Grand Trunk of 1777 and the 1820's. Johnson wisely invested in this novelty, securing his servant Frank's annuity on the profits of Langton's 'navigation'. The Industrial Revolution went forward for many years on water power, which was used for Richard Arkwright's factory on the Derwent (1771) and for the Darby's enlarged iron-works at Coalbrooksdale, whose spread was lamented by Anna Seward, the Swan of Lichfield, in a poem of about 1785.[2] The mills were still countryfied, light and almost angelic, like Wedgwood's Etruria, although the true steam age was not far off. Between 1775 and 1800 Bolton and Watt built 321 steam engines, hardly enough to pollute the air of new factory towns but a token of the greatness and misery to come. Johnson, who was cautiously benevolent to all such technical progress, even lived into the air age. In 1784 he wrote to Hector, 'I did not reach Oxford until Friday morning, and then I sent Francis to see the balloon fly, but could not go myself. . . .' On Friday, 12th November, James Sadler of Oxford, the first English aeronaut, made his second flight.

Johnson's travels and observations of mankind, in the last years of his life, are soon told. After Thrale's death he was busy for a while as an executor, 'bustling about, with an ink-horn and pen in his button-hole, like an excise-man' as he negotiated a profitable sale of the brewery to Barclay and Perkins. In June he went with Boswell

[1] *An Economic History of England in the Eighteenth Century*, 1955.
[2] W. G. Hoskins, *The Making of the English Landscape*, 1955.

to Southill in Bedfordshire, and in the autumn of 1781 he made his usual round trip to Oxford, Birmingham, Lichfield, and Ashbourne. In the winter of 1781 his health became much worse. Mrs Thrale spent much time looking after him, in Bolt Court and her London house; she was as kind as ever, but was beginning to find his dependence on her irksome. In May 1782 he was able to start his visits to Streatham again, and in August to work on the revision of the *Lives*, which was published in the following year. When Mrs Thrale told him of her plan to take her family abroad, he received the news calmly; expecting him to be upset, she was hurt. In October he took leave of Streatham, which was to be sold, and spent six unhappy weeks with Mrs Thrale at Brighton. By this time the *Morning Post* was talking of his possible marriage with Mrs Thrale, but she was thinking only of Piozzi, the amiable Italian musician with whom she was now deeply in love.

Johnson spent another wretched winter, writing on 11th December: 'My life being unsettled between Argyle Street [where Mrs Thrale had rented a house] and Bolt Court, my body disordered, and opium frequently taken.' In January 1783 the antagonism between Mrs Thrale and her daughters about Piozzi reached a crisis, and Piozzi agreed to go abroad. There were comments in the newspapers, and rumours which must have reached Johnson. In March, Boswell found him depressed and irritable, and on 5th April he wrote in his diary: 'I took leave of Mrs Thrale. I was much moved. I had some expostulations with her. She said that she was likewise affected. I commended the Thrales with great good will to God; may my petitions have been heard!' Mrs Thrale went off to Bath and he was not to see her again, although he wrote often to her and to her daughter Queeny, describing his symptoms in detail. It is striking that the majority of Johnson's extant letters date from the last three years of his life: letter-writing, in which he had long been perfunctory or businesslike, had become his means of holding on to life. His hold was precarious, for as he wrote in his diary under 16th June: 'I went to bed, and, as I conceive, about 3 in the morning, I had a stroke of the palsy.' He soon recovered and made two trips that summer, to Rochester and to Wiltshire. He was within a few miles of Weymouth, where Mrs Thrale was staying, but aware that her sympathy was waning, made no attempt to see her. During that autumn Mrs Thrale became hysterically ill, through longing for Piozzi; her hard-hearted daughters relented and Piozzi was sent for, although he could not get back from Italy until the next spring. Meanwhile Johnson had spent another wretched winter. The weather was severe, and this aggravated his chronic bronchitis and consequently his heart disease; he went on describing his health to Mrs Thrale, whose mind was otherwise occupied. After her rapturous reunion with Piozzi, Mrs Thrale wrote at the end of June 1784 from Bath to all Thrale's executors, with a special message to Johnson, to announce her intended remarriage. Johnson replied in a terrible outburst of bitterness:

> Madam July 2, 1784
>
> If I interpret your letter right, you are ignominiously married, if it is yet undone, let us once more talk together. If you have abandoned your children and your religion, God forgive your wickedness; if you have forfeited your Fame, and your country, may your folly do no further mischief.
>
> If the last act is yet to do, I, who have loved you, esteemed you, reverenced you, and served you, I who long thought you the first of human kind, entreat that before your fate is irrevocable, I may once more see you. I was, I once was,
>
> Madam, most truly yours, SAM. JOHNSON
>
> I will come down if you will permit it.

Mrs Thrale wrote back with spirit and dignity to defend her conduct and Piozzi's character; and on 8th July Johnson wrote to her again, in more restrained and kindly terms, but still urging her to think again about marriage. There was no more correspondence between them; four months later, when the Piozzis were enjoying a gay tour of the Continent, Johnson told Fanny Burney, 'I drive her quite out of my mind'.

Not long before the break with Mrs Thrale he had dined at the Club and said good-bye to Boswell, each for the last time. He expected death but went on fighting for life. Unable to describe his symptoms to Mrs Thrale, he wrote them down in a gruesome Latin diary which he called *Aegri Ephemeris*, which also records the pain he inflicted on himself by his resolute amateur doctoring. He wrote many letters to other friends, mainly about his own physical state, but still showing flashes of wit and of interest in the world around him. He made a last long trip to Oxford, Lichfield, Birmingham, and Ashbourne, in order to set his financial affairs in order; in November he returned from Lichfield to London, prepared to die. He feared death but faced it with courage, saying towards the end, 'I will be conquered, I will not capitulate.' On the 13th of December at the beginning of another bitter winter he died.

The post-mortem examination showed that he had suffered from bronchitis and emphysema (abnormal inflation produced by air in the cellular tissue of the lungs), which would account for his famous puffing and blowing, as well as for his heart disease. A drawing of his lungs was used as a plate in Clift's *Morbid Anatomy*, the earliest textbook on pathology: Johnson would have been glad to be of such service to medicine. He had survived to the age of seventy-five only by the heroic application of his will-power; and it would be wrong to attribute his death to his sufferings over Mrs Thrale. It would probably also be wrong to exaggerate the strength of his emotional bond with her, or to say as some have done that he was 'in love' with her. His outburst was caused by the irritations of old age (which is just another name for terminal disease): by the knowledge that he would be deprived of Mrs Thrale's attentions as nurse, companion, and correspondent; and by his feeling of responsibility towards her. As one of Thrale's executors he had been left in a position of trust, and he had genuine fears about Piozzi's intentions, since Piozzi was a relatively penniless musician and Mrs Thrale an heiress—this was the age of adventurers in marriage. Mrs Thrale's daughters and most of her friends were equally hostile to the match. Johnson had also a deep veneration for the memory of Henry Thrale, and his feelings must have been coloured by the realization that Mrs Thrale had always been indifferent to her husband. The break was painful but not tragic; and it should be the verdict of history that both Johnson and Mrs Thrale stand acquitted of selfish cruelty.

The purpose of this study, however, is not to give an explanation of Johnson's character, or to convey the flavour of his personality—what need for the latter, since it is revealed so perfectly in the pages of Boswell? I have tried, rather, to show how Johnson stood in relation to his own age; and I must now try to say what he means, or could mean, to ours. His greatest and most enduring work seems to me, in the last analysis, to be his contribution to wisdom. From all his writings, not only the *Rambler* but his letters, literary criticism, parliamentary reporting, and from his recorded conversation, there can be drawn a body of maxims and apothegms which concentrate his experience and reflection into memorable words. Because readers have felt these sayings to be a helpful guide to living, several collections of them have been made since his death.[1] When his work is excerpted and rearranged suitably, it can be seen to have strong affinities with the ancient tradition technically known as 'Wisdom Literature'. This is a genre distinct from that of the proverb, which is a product of folk-lore and offers the practical teaching of peasant culture. Wisdom Literature springs from a more advanced civilization, and is written by and for the 'clerks' or *literati* of such a civilization. The earliest example seems to be the maxims of the vizier Ptah-hotep of Fifth-dynasty Egypt which are directives for a successful life in the service of the Pharaoh. This and later Egyptian compilations, less purely prudential, have left traces in the Hebrew Book of Proverbs (which are not proverbs in the strict sense but belong to Wisdom Literature). But even the Biblical Proverbs have the double focus characteristic of ancient Egyptian wisdom: both on to the values of courtly society and on to the higher values of ethics and religion. The Proverbs point at both worldly and unworldly ends: on the one hand, they tell you how to speak tactfully before a king, or how to make a good marriage; on the other hand, they inculcate the fear of the Lord and the love of righteousness. This mixture of the prudential and the ethical characterizes most of the other examples of this genre, whether by Confucius, Marcus Aurelius, Bacon, Addison, Pope, or Johnson himself. La Rochefoucauld is too cynical to be squarely in the tradition, Sir Thomas Browne (whose *Christian Morals* was much admired by Johnson) and Epictetus perhaps too other-worldly. Epictetus at his most practical has, however, left a trace on Johnson's thought:

> Two things must be rooted out of man: conceit and diffidence. Conceit lies in thinking you want nothing; and diffidence in supposing it impossible that under such adverse circumstances you should succeed.
> —(D. iii.14, 4)

> A request made with diffidence and timidity is easily denied, because the petitioner himself seems to doubt its fitness.—(*Rambler* 166)

[1] The latest and most conveniently arranged is *The Wisdom of Dr. Johnson*, compiled by Constantia Maxwell, 1948.

Johnson delighted in this crisp mode of conveying ideas, saying, 'I fancy mankind may come, in time, to write all aphoristically'. He seems to be closest of all to the Biblical Proverbs and to the similar parts of Ecclesiastes, which in its world-weary serenity is the inspiration of *Rasselas*. Sometimes Johnson's phraseology has the very ring of Proverbs. 'Wisdom is the principal thing, therefore get wisdom: and with all thy getting get understanding' suggests two famous remarks: 'every man gets as much Greek as he can', and to a stupid disputant, 'Sir, I have found you an argument; but I am not obliged to find you an understanding'. Like the Biblical authors Johnson often distilled his wisdom into a poetic image. Just as the dog returns to his vomit, the thorns crackle under a pot, or a quarrelling wife is a continual dropping of rain, so in Johnson 'Sorrow is a kind of rust of the soul', and a fool is a fellow 'rattling a rattle-box, only don't let him think that he thunders'.

In content even more than in style Johnson is close to the central tradition. It is remarkable how little distance he puts between the ethical and the prudential. His first assumption is that the good life is to be lived in the normal context of society; compare Marcus Aurelius, 'every action of thine must tend to the perfection of a life that is truly sociable'. The sphere of wisdom includes for Johnson such things as eating ('I look upon it, that he who does not mind his belly will hardly mind anything else'), money ('there are few ways in which a man can be more innocently employed than in getting money'), and good manners. If Johnson's own manners at table or on meeting strangers were not always of the highest polish, he nevertheless insisted that this was an important topic, as in the *Rambler*: 'When once the forms of civility are violated, there remains little hope of return to kindness or decency.' (55); 'There are many arts of graciousness and conciliation, which are to be practised without expense, and by which those may be made our friends, who have never received from us any real benefit.' The latter might be a quotation from the letters of Johnson's *bête noire* Lord Chesterfield, so practical is its emphasis on success in life; and Chesterfield might have wished he had been the first to say, 'there are people whom one should like very well to drop, but would not wish to be dropped by'.

On a higher level, Johnson often insists on *mens sana in corpore sano*. If it is cant to suppose that the good life can be lived in solitude or poverty, it is common sense to advise that it cannot be lived without health. Johnson may have been 'very sincere in good principles, without having good practice'; perhaps he took exercise only when Thrale made him take it, but he eloquently asked his readers to consider 'how much happiness is gained, and how much misery escaped, by frequent and violent agitation of the body'. As for mental health, he spoke from the experience of a lifetime's struggle to hold on to his sanity. Especially in the pages of Boswell, who was himself a sufferer from various mental ills, there are many pages of good counsel on how to divert melancholy, by study, conversation and company, in fact 'by every means but drinking'.

Most of Johnson's apothegms are concerned with daily life in its social and domestic setting; with the problems of marriage, children, friendship, youth and age, sorrows and pleasures. When he goes beyond such things to consider the higher realms of ethics and religion, he is usually disappointing, not because there is any trace of insincerity, but because his spiritual life is too earthbound, his sense of human possibilities too limited. 'Of him that hopes to be forgiven, it is indispensably required that he forgive. It is therefore superfluous to urge any other motive' is a noble saying, but poetically weak besides the Gospels. His ethics are utilitarian, and his highest appeal is to the Stoic concept of duty, as he propounds it in *Rasselas*: 'all skill ought to be exerted for universal good; every man has owed much to others, and ought to repay the kindness that he has received'. Since Stoic and utilitarian ideals are the best basis for decent living, all this is admirable; but nothing in Johnson has the imaginative insight of the greatest aphorists, like Blake or Nietzsche.

To a moralist of Johnson's stamp, education is the most important duty. Does not Marcus Aurelius say 'either teach them or bear with them'? Johnson devoted much thought to the teaching of children, in the spirit of Proverbs 22:6, 'Train up a child in the way he should go; and when he is old, he will not depart from it':

> Accustom your children constantly to this; if a thing happened at one window, and they when relating it, say that it happened at another, do not let it pass, but instantly check them; you do not know where deviation from truth will end.

For most of his life, however, he was a teacher of mature men, who found his teaching acceptable. Everything Johnson says appears to have been tested in his own life; as Ian Watt said in a memorable bicentenary broadcast, this is 'the literature of experience'. Experience goes with immense learning, which he wore lightly ('Books without the knowledge of life are useless; for what should books teach but the art of living?'), and with shrewdness in the analysis of character; and all are combined with formal wit. Such an epigram as 'All censure of a man's self is oblique praise. It is in order to show how much he can spare' gives at once the delights of surprise and of truth, and leads the reader to self-examination. Like many of his sayings it is ironical, and reflects his lack of illusions about his fellow-men, but it is not cynical. Johnson never like the cynic turns his back on the richness of life. Finally he speaks with the authority of one who has made himself into a complete man; after a life of suffering and struggle, his words of comfort come from the depth of an integrated being.

'Then hath a man attained to the estate of perfection in his life and conversation, when he spends every day, as if it were his last day.' Johnson, who so often reproached himself with wasting time and feared that the end would find him unprepared, would nevertheless deserve the praise of Marcus Aurelius as much as any man. His conversation was always near perfection, his charity never failed. 'Johnson is dead,' said his friend Hamilton.—'Let us go to the next best:—there is nobody;—no man can be said to put you in mind of Johnson.' He died a national institution and a friend to many; and he has remained both ever since. He was a maker of Britain in that he was a founder of our lexicography and literary criticism; and as poet and author of *Rasselas* he takes his place in national literary history, of which he was the first great historian. But as a teacher of wisdom he has done even more: he has sharpened the wits of many generations and helped to clear their minds of cant. In many of his opinions and prejudices, religious, political, or critical, he belongs to the dead past; in his tolerance, energy, and intelligence he belongs to a world which is still possible.

INDEX

The numerals in **heavy type** refer to the figure numbers of illustrations.